Live Well, Learn Well

A practical approach to supporting student wellbeing

Abigail Mann

BLOOMSBURY EDUCATION

LONDON OXFORD NEW YORK NEW DELHI SYDNEY

BLOOMSBURY EDUCATION
Bloomsbury Publishing Plc
50 Bedford Square, London, WC1B 3DP, UK

BLOOMSBURY, BLOOMSBURY EDUCATION and the Diana logo are trademarks
of Bloomsbury Publishing Plc

First published in Great Britain, 2020

A catalogue record for this book is available from the British Library

ISBN: PB: 978-1-4729-7225-5; ePDF: 978-1-4729-7224-8; ePub: 978-1-4729-7227-9

2 4 6 8 10 9 7 5 3 1 (paperback)

Typeset by Newgen KnowledgeWorks Pvt. Ltd., Chennai, India
Printed and bound in the UK by CPI Group (UK) Ltd, Croydon, CR0 4YY

Contents

Chapter 3: Soothe away stress

Chapter 4: Learning legends

Chapter 5: Rocking revision

Chapter 6: Super citizens   115

Chapter 7: Whole-school student wellbeing   135

Acknowledgements

To all contributors on Twitter, to friends with suggestions, to the awesome hive mind that is the Litdrive group, and to Martyn Reah (@MartynReah) and the #teacher5aday folk, I thank you from the bottom of my heart. Without your support, I wouldn't have got there. I am truly grateful.

To my publishers, in particular my editor, Hannah. Thank you for giving me another opportunity to share my ideas. And thank you for your patience!

To the staff and students at Whitefield School, in particular the incredible English department, thank you for making Whitefield such a welcoming, supportive and wonderful place to work. To the Whitefield besties, Claire, Erika, Aanisah, Evi and Tan, thank you for always flying my flag. I'm forever indebted.

For the ladies in my life: Laura, Katherine, Nicola, Hayley, Rhea, Rachel, Beka, Anissa and Amy. A force of womanhood I'm proud to hold dear.

For the sisterhood: Rochelle, Zoe, Kaitlin, Emma and Hannah. I burst with pride at all you do.

For Dad: quite possibly indestructible. I'm still running like the wind. Thank you for always being there.

For Mum: the kindest woman and soul I have ever met. Thank you for all that you are and all that you do.

'Each time a woman stands up for herself, without knowing it possibly, without claiming it, she stands up for all women.' Maya Angelou.

Introduction

Every now and then, I pinch myself to check that this world of authoring is one in which I actually reside. After the success of my first book, *Live Well, Teach Well*, which surprisingly became a number one bestseller on Amazon, I felt that my journey in the world of writing was only just beginning. I still had many ideas buzzing around my head from which I felt many educators and students could benefit. It's remarkable how much one's teaching practice can develop and transform over the years. With that transformation comes new approaches, fine-tuned teaching pedagogy and for me, a passion for teaching ignited over and over again. I truly love my job and all that it encompasses, from teaching English, to leading a team and working with the most incredible, motivated, ambitious and friendly young people I have ever met. I consider it a true privilege to be able to make a difference every day. So, it was with renewed gusto and great pleasure that I submitted another book proposal to Bloomsbury, this time with a sharp focus on student wellbeing.

Students in today's education system are feeling the pressure; there is no doubt about that. In 2018, the NHS released new statistics that painted a depressing picture. One in eight (12.8 per cent) children and young people aged between five and 19 have a diagnosable mental health condition. The prevalence of five- to 15-year-olds experiencing emotional disorders (including anxiety and depression) has increased by 48 per cent – from 3.9 per cent in 2004 to 5.8 per cent in 2017. A third (34.9 per cent) of the young people aged 14 to 19 years old who identified as lesbian, gay, bisexual or with another sexual identity had a mental health condition, as opposed to 13.2 per cent of those who identified as heterosexual. Only a quarter (25.2 per cent) of five- to 19-year-olds with a mental health condition had contact with mental health specialists in the past year, meaning that three-quarters hadn't had any contact with mental health services. Whilst schools are not mental health services, they do have a duty of care towards the students they serve and, as such, should be doing what they can to ensure all young people leave the education system happy and successful. This book goes some way towards ensuring that aim is both seriously considered and successfully met.

The book is split into seven chapters, all designed to promote student wellbeing. In each of them, you will find practical ideas to support young people as individuals and as a collective student body. The chapters cover: individual student wellbeing; how to encourage students to recognise the wellbeing of others and how to recognise students' efforts as a teacher; effective methods to destress young people; how to improve the learning journey for students in your class; tried and tested revision strategies; how to encourage students to be super citizens; and finally, ideas about whole-school student wellbeing.

I suggest you use the book as a 'pick up and look' resource for when you need it most. For example, if you are dealing with some very anxious students, the chapter titled 'Sooth away stress' can help you. If you are looking to develop wellbeing on a larger scale, the chapters titled 'Whole-school student wellbeing' or 'Super citizens' can support you with this.

I write the final edits of this book five weeks into the UK's nationwide school closure in spring and summer 2020 due to the coronavirus outbreak. During this time, as usual, teachers have risen to the challenge of a new way of teaching. Almost instantly, scores of lesson resources were made by teachers to support teachers. Online video platforms were navigated and successfully installed. A plethora of superb online CPD opportunities was made available and continues to grow by the day. Teachers across the country are calling their students weekly to check on their wellbeing. It is times like these that make me feel phenomenally proud to be part of such a resilient, organised and empathetic profession. I hope my offering goes some way to supporting teachers during what is likely to be a very stormy time in education for both teachers and students alike. I would love to know how useful the book has been for you, so please feel free to tag your comments on Twitter using the hashtags at the end of each idea.

From one devoted teacher, sanguine with the hope that the teaching profession will one day be sustainable for everyone, to another: I hope you find it useful.

Chapter 1

Winning wellbeing

Without first tackling their own personal wellbeing, it can be difficult for students to focus on their learning. This chapter is filled with ideas to support them with this.

It isn't hard to notice the current statistics surrounding young people and mental health. In 2004, a survey found that one in five people aged five to 15 had a mental health disorder. This figure rose to one in nine by 2017. If we increase the age range to five to 19, the figure rises again to one in eight. The reason for the rise in the figure is an increase in emotional disorders, including anxiety and depression. Young people today are more affected by these than ever before. We are not health care professionals, but as educators we have a responsibility to care for the students in our charge, both academically and emotionally. This chapter goes some small way to supporting the wellbeing needs of the students we teach.

With a focus on individual wellbeing, this chapter is packed with ideas to support young people. From advice about achieving a healthy balance, to building effective relationships between staff and students and ensuring your classroom is a calm and welcoming environment in which to learn, you can find plenty here to get you started. There are also ideas about your own attitude as teachers and how to ensure this is kept positive to have the best effect on the young people we serve. Dive in and try out something new with your students. I'd love to know how you get on!

Idea 1: The 5-a-day challenge

Five a day keeps the stress at bay.

One way to encourage students to focus on their own wellbeing is to introduce the 5-a-day challenge. This idea was developed from the original teacher-5-a-day blog Martyn Reah shared. The five strands originate from the New Economics Foundation Centre for Wellbeing: https://issuu.com/neweconomicsfoundation/docs/five_ways_to_well-being. If you have never heard of teacher-5-a-day before, I suggest you start by looking at Martyn's blog: www.martynreah.wordpress.com. It's packed with ideas to support wellbeing. The five key areas to support personal wellbeing are: exercise, notice, connect, learn and volunteer.

By encouraging students to focus on these key areas, you will be ensuring they work on their own personal balance, but also their ability to reflect on their day and recognise the world around them. Here are a few ideas you could suggest to your students:

Exercise:

- Walk to school instead of catching the bus.
- At break, walk the perimeter of the school grounds.
- Take the long route to the classroom (as long as you remind them about punctuality!).
- Take part in extracurricular activities.
- Lead a sports session for younger students.

Notice:

- Notice something different on your way to school.
- Travel a different route home.
- Notice and acknowledge when someone does something for you that wasn't required but they did it anyway.
- Notice when you are feeling negative or stressed and act upon it.
- Notice when others are feeling negative or stressed and try to help them.

Connect:

- Speak to someone you would not normally come into contact with. Ask them how they are. This could be another student, the dinner staff, or even a teacher.
- Email your teacher if you are stuck on a task and need some more support. They are there to help.
- Connect with someone in your community. Do you have neighbours? Are they elderly? Do they need support?
- Connect with another school and become pen pals with a student there.
- Call someone you have not spoken to in a while and catch up.

Learn:

- Spend 20 minutes reading today.
- Put 100 per cent effort into every subject today.
- Discover five facts about a topic with which you are struggling.
- Watch a documentary about something you are interested in.
- Complete your homework on the day it is set to keep the information fresh in your mind.

Volunteer:

- Offer to support your teacher with some classroom tasks.
- Give some of your time to become a club or sports leader.
- Volunteer to support younger students with their reading.
- Support at home by volunteering to do chores.

There are, of course, plenty more ideas you could include and the possibilities are endless. The main thing to remember is that you are encouraging students to focus on their own wellbeing and perhaps be more reflective of their choices as an outcome.

Next steps

If you are unsure about trying the 5-a-day model, why not try a 5-a-week model instead? Encourage students to focus on one of the strands each day before eventually aiming for the 5-a-day approach.

#5adaychallenge
#personalwellbeing

Idea 2: Staff versus students

Building relationships with students and staff alike encourages community spirit.

A good way to focus on wellbeing and nurture great relationships between staff and students is to create a series of competitions across the year. The model below is an example based on teacher-5-a-day.

Term 1: #volunteer
In the first term, time spent volunteering is clocked up, and students and staff compete directly with each other. At the end of the term, the winners are announced and prizes won. Examples of volunteering could be a teacher taking a colleague's lesson or a student helping a peer with their work. Volunteering outside of school should count too.

Term 2: #learn
Take part in the 'Great <insert school name> Knowledge Quiz'. This could be tailored to a particular subject or theme. I've done this with the whole school taking part during tutor time; it was a real talking point as tutor groups tried to figure out the answers. Other ideas include a competition for the best 100-word story, poem or even song.

Term 3: #exercise
The sporty one. Staff versus students <insert sporting activity here>. A great way to boost mid-year lethargy.

Term 4: #connect
This idea could be anything from an internet or app competition, to a cross-curricular event. The term #connect refers to making connections whether that be using technology or simply joining people together.

Term 5: #notice
Staff and students catch people doing good deeds. They add names of those 'caught' to a 'notice' box. The winning side will be the team with the most names in the box and you can share all the good deeds in an assembly.

Term 6: #celebrate
After all the competitions, celebrate the winners in a final assembly.

#teachervstudent

Idea 3: Class mascot

Having a class mascot promotes positivity.

Over the years, I have accrued many mascots, but one in particular has remained a firm favourite with students.

Around seven years ago I came across a little stuffed toy in a garden centre. He caught my eye because of his insanely huge grin. He came with this message: 'May his joyful smile remind you of all there is to be happy about.' I couldn't resist him. That little pig is now the infamous 'Pig of Happiness' that has resided in my classroom since that day. He has provided support to students in more ways than I ever thought he would. Firstly, he actually came with a video on YouTube all about how to spread happiness, which I regularly show the students. It's old-fashioned, but they like it. Secondly, if anyone is feeling a little down or deflated he becomes their mascot for the lesson. He sits on their desk with his ridiculous grin and they return his smile. In my experience this works with any age group, even sixth formers! He's an instant mood lifter. Thirdly, he's often a stimulant for their work. Narratives have involved him. Crime scenes have revolved around him. He even has friends in the form of other stuffed animals. It needs to be mentioned that it hasn't always been easy for him. Some students (and teachers) have found it funny to kidnap him and send me horrifying images!

This anecdote goes to show how a class mascot can impact wellbeing: they can be used to improve the mood of your class as well as provide impetus for learning.

Next steps

Get a mascot for your department, house or school and use it to promote healthy competition and positive behaviour. Classes can compete to have the mascot reside in their classroom for the week by winning the most house points or having the best overall attendance, for example.

Loan the mascot to students, offering individuals the chance to take it home for the weekend or a half-term break. They could take pictures of where the mascot has travelled and what activities it has taken part in. This instils responsibility and subtly develops trust between teachers and students.

#classmascot
#connect
#mascottravels

Idea 4: Logging the love

Fiona Jarret, English teacher at Rawlins Academy, Loughborough, writes about encouraging students to keep a log of supportive notes, cards or comments they receive.

We receive more communication in the modern world than ever before. Between Instagram, TikTok, Snapchat and other messaging services, the number of messages we receive daily can easily run into the hundreds. We hear constant reports of how damaging all this interaction is, but with so many of us reaching out for support and friendship through technology instead of face to face, there's usually a whole lot of love and care being exchanged too. This support can easily go unrecorded: even the most special of messages can get lost in a sea of notifications and updates. Are your students taking time to really appreciate what others are saying?

Keeping a message log

The aim of this simple idea is to encourage students to take time to record the messages that make them smile or touch their heart.

Ask students to find somewhere to keep their special messages. It could be a notebook or a glass jar. Each time they get a message that brings a smile to their face or cheers them up on a tough day, ask them to take a moment to write it down. If they're busy or not at home, they could take screenshots of special messages so they are easy to locate later. They could also write down nice things their parents or teachers say.

When they're having a difficult day, or are feeling lost or stressed, ask them to open their notebook or jar. They will enjoy reading those messages and it will remind them of how much support they have around them. They could even contact the sender of one of the messages and pass their smile on.

Next steps

Encourage students to create entire scrapbooks of cards, notes and photos of each of their secondary school years. This would be a lasting keepsake for years to come.

**#logoflove
#rainyday
keepsake**

Idea 5: The water challenge

Hydrated students are healthier and more likely to perform well in their studies.

The benefits of drinking water have long been known to all, but even today our students choose sugar-filled energy drinks over a simple glass of water. As teachers acting *in loco parentis*, we have a responsibility to ensure that our students make the right choices in life and drinking their body weight in sugary drinks isn't one of them. Drinking eight glasses of water a day can yield these benefits:

1. It supports the functioning of your body, which is 60 per cent water.
2. It supports muscle stamina. Muscles feel tired if you're dehydrated.
3. It helps with digestion. Your body needs water to support the flow of food through your digestive system.
4. It supports weight loss. Drinking water before a meal encourages your body to think it is full quicker, which prevents overeating. With obesity statistics on the rise, this is important. Water has also been shown in studies to speed up metabolism.
5. It keeps skin clear. Hydration helps to flush out unwanted toxins – great news for students wishing for a glowing complexion.
6. It relieves fatigue. If you are dehydrated your body has to work harder, causing you to feel tired.
7. It fights illness. The common cold can be fought off more quickly if your body is hydrated.
8. It boosts brain power. When you are dehydrated, your brain slows down. Staying hydrated keeps your mind sharp and active.

With all of these benefits, it should be easy to encourage students to drink more water. Why not introduce a water challenge to your form time? Create a tally chart with each student's name down the left-hand column. Add eight further columns numbered one to eight along the top, representing eight glasses of water. Each morning, students tally their water consumption from the previous day. Reward students who achieve their daily target of eight glasses to promote the same positive healthy behaviours again. Include your own name on the chart. Modelling the behaviour you wish to see is hugely important in gaining student buy-in.

#thewaterchallenge

Idea 6: Weather makers

Your attitude in the classroom can make or break a lesson.

It is often heard in schools that students can be livelier and more disruptive when it's windy. Whether there's any truth in that or not is yet to be significantly researched. What might be better to accurately report is that your behaviour and attitude in the classroom can and will impact on the behaviour of the students in your class. School teacher, child psychologist and psychotherapist, Haim G. Ginott stated:

'I've come to a frightening conclusion that I am the decisive element in the classroom. It's my personal approach that creates the climate. It's my daily mood that makes the weather. As a teacher, I possess a tremendous power to make a child's life miserable or joyous.'

It makes perfect sense to me that whatever mood I am in, I must show up every day and offer the same relentless positivity that my students deserve. Here are some consistent approaches you can try, to ensure that, however you feel that day, you manage to pull off that positivity.

- **Smile:** Smile, smile and smile again. Even if you really don't feel like it. Smiling makes you feel good. It releases neuropeptides that fight off stress, which in turn releases dopamine, endorphins and serotonin. All of these things lower heart rate and blood pressure and improve your mood. Smiling also makes others feel good too. Smiling is actually contagious! The part of your brain that is responsible for your facial expression of smiling when happy or mimicking another's smile resides in the cingulate cortex, an unconscious automatic response area. When people are smiled at, it is an automatic response to smile back. So, by smiling at your students, you are sharing that feel-good mood released when you smile yourself.
- **Greet them at the door:** This is so important if you want to start the lesson off positively. If you are busying yourself at the desk whilst your students enter the room, the chances are they will enter haphazardly in dribs and drabs, chatting away and will soon become distracted by each other. To avoid this, be ready. Stand at the door, greet every one of your students with a hello and a welcome and direct them to the entry task you have prepared.

- **Ask them about their day:** Ask them how they are. Enquire about their weekend. And mean it. If students know you care about their wellbeing, they are far more likely to work hard for you in your lessons.
- **Say thank you:** It can be easy to forget this in the throes of a busy lesson. If a student offers to hand out the books, thank them. If a student offers a response in class, thank them. If a student offers to collect resources, thank them. I can't emphasise this enough. Students love to be recognised for their efforts and a simple thank you really does go a long way.
- **Notice the little things:** Neat exercise book? Tell them. Homework handed in early? Acknowledge it. Extra effort in class? Let them know you have noticed. Everyone likes to feel appreciated, so why not ensure your students are too?
- **Be firm, but fair:** Students tend to have a very strong sense of justice. They notice if another student is being treated differently to them. Aim to be as fair as possible when dealing with your students. And be consistently firm with your rules and boundaries. That way, students know where they stand and feel safe and comfortable in your classroom.
- **Recognise their success:** If they have been successful in their learning, tell them. Praise them to others too. All too often those who always get it right can be overlooked and their success becomes the norm. They still deserve to be praised in a way that they appreciate.
- **Give them a voice:** Allow students to contribute to the lesson in a way that suits them. Get to know them so you can decide how this might work. Students who have had the opportunity to contribute to the lesson in some way will feel more valued in that lesson.
- **Dismiss them calmly:** Just as you begin the lesson by greeting them at the door and welcoming them in, it is equally as important to calmly dismiss the class too. Students love routine. If your lessons begin and end positively and sensibly, they will remember this and begin to think of your classroom as a positive environment to be in. And don't forget that smile!

Next steps

Why not pick out one or two of the ideas above, try them out for a term and then reflect on the outcome? If they've worked, try a couple more! Before you know it, those marginal gains you have acquired will have changed the weather in your classroom.

#weathermakers
#positiveclassroom
#notice

Idea 7: Creativity challenge

Allowing students the chance to be creative encourages enthusiasm and promotes wellbeing.

Every so often, I like to give students a homework task that allows them to be creative. It's a chance for them to demonstrate their understanding, or even to simply engage with a topic in a way they feel comfortable with. Teaching in the English classroom is full of academic rigour and challenging writing activities. The homework project allows some freedom of expression they would not normally have in the classroom. Why not try this in your own subject too and give students a choice of activities to complete? Here are some ideas:

- **Cakes:** Students love to bake. In the past, I have received cake models of the Globe Theatre and even World War One trenches. Baking tasks would work well for subjects like science where students could demonstrate understanding of cells, for example.
- **Poems:** Encourage students to demonstrate their understanding by writing a poem. Obviously this works well in English lessons, but it's also a great way to demonstrate any knowledge, particularly in history, geography or RE.
- **Songs:** These work in the same way as poems but have the added bonus of being sung in lessons, which always generates a few smiles.
- **Costumes:** Ask students to design or make costumes for characters in books they are studying in English or drama.
- **Imagery tasks:** Many students like to recreate scenes from books or plays using their own images. This idea can be covered in subjects like art and could be a cross-curricular task.
- **Models:** Some students go to great lengths to create shoebox models of scenes from the books we have read. Subjects like history could easily apply this idea to recall significant events.

What you will notice with all these activities is the sheer amount of pride students display when they bring their completed projects in. Just remember to be sensitive to the fact that some students may not have the resources for all these tasks at home, so be careful when you assign them.

#creativitychaos
#learn
#connect

Idea 8: Nature nurture

Encouraging students to care for something improves their sense of responsibility.

This year, I gave my form tutees a small planting tray and some seeds and told them to care for them. I decided not to tell them what each of their seeds were to add to the surprise when they finally bloom into beautiful flowers. The students were so excited about the prospect of growing something of their own. Often, they turn up early to water their plants and it's a real joy to see them take so much time and consideration over something.

Benefits of growing plants

- **Sensory development:** Planting engages all the senses and students will recognise them without even thinking about it. They use the sense of touch when they feel the plants, soil, seeds and petals.
- **Responsibility and patience:** Students improve these two qualities as they come to understand that something else is dependent upon their care for its survival. Growing any kind of plant requires daily care and attention and students will have to wait to see the fruits of their labour. They have to remain engaged in the task of watering the plants even if they cannot see any visible progress or gain.
- **Social skills:** Spending time with other form group members growing plants helps to develop students' social skills. They learn to work together, sharing responsibilities such as fetching the water and checking to see if the soil is damp. They bond as they begin to see each flower grow and congratulate each other on their success.
- **Mood and wellbeing:** Growing plants has been known to improve your mood, productivity, concentration and creativity. Having plants in the classroom also impacts on the wellbeing of all those who use the room. They have been known to reduce stress. They also clean the air to make it free from toxins.

Next steps
Why not take a visit to your local garden centre and pick up some planting trays to begin your planting journey with your class? Before you know it, your classroom will be the jungle every child deserves to see.

#naturenurture
#growth
#resilience

Idea 9: Know your *Optimus Prime*

Teaching students about their own energy levels and habits saves them time.

Students must be taught the importance of recognising their best working hours and when they are least productive. It is our responsibility to ensure students know their wellbeing can be affected by poor learning habits. These ideas are just some of the ways this topic can be broached.

- **Ask students to identify when they are most productive with school work outside of normal school hours.** They may find this difficult, so ask them to trial both morning and evening sessions. Whatever time they identify should be the time they build into their week for completing homework or revision.
- **Share tips with students about how to stay on top of homework or revision.** Jill Berry, a former headteacher and school advisor, often mentions the phrase, 'eating the frog.' What she means by this is to undertake the difficult tasks first and then anything after that seems easy. Advise students to manage their time effectively in the same way.
- **Share practical tips on how to stay focused and not overload yourself.** Many of the students I teach try to go at revision or learning all guns blazing and before they know it, they are exhausted and stressed. They must be taught how to balance their time. Revision timetables that build incrementally are perfect for this.
- **Advise students to create an effective learning space for themselves.** This could be a place at home, but it doesn't have to be. Libraries are a wonderful learning space. They are quiet, calm, spacious and filled with knowledge.
- **Advise students to learn or revise together.** Often, topics can be broken down if more than one person is reviewing them. This has the added benefit of developing working groups and friendships.

If students know their most productive time and develop effective habits, they are happier when learning and make excellent progress.

#optimusprime
#learn

Idea 10: Resource ready

Having a fully stocked resource cupboard allows for creative teaching ideas in class.

Once the exciting content of my lessons is planned, I turn to the tools I have at my disposal to further engage students. Part of taking care of student wellbeing is ensuring they enjoy learning. This can be achieved with a variety of teaching tools, including the following.

- **Sticky notes:** These are cheap, colourful and easy to use, whether it be for assessment, planning or creating connections between ideas. They can be stuck anywhere, from your whiteboard to your windows.
- **Timers and bells:** A whole variety of timers live in my classroom – sand ones, liquid ones, even giant bombs. They are useful for quizzes and tasks that need to be timed for pace. I also have three service bells that we use in a similar way as time warnings or as prompts for students to change activities.
- **Pegs:** These are great for timelines, ordering events, justifying ideas and for hanging up exemplary student work.
- **Poster paper:** Use this for making huge revision mind maps. Students work together using only their minds to create them. They're great visuals and are best displayed in the corridor as they are so big!
- **Glass pens:** These are great for adding a bit of variety to your lessons. You can use them to write on windows, but also on desks as the ink washes off easily. Students absolutely love them.
- **Mini-whiteboards:** Use these for low-stakes quizzes at the beginning of a lesson to test students on previous knowledge. They are great because you get instant feedback on students' understanding.

This is not an exhaustive list but even if you try a few of these props out with your class, it will create a positive environment for your students and will encourage imagination in your classes.

Next steps

Consider how you can promote engagement in your lessons. What items would the students find most interesting? How would they add value to the learning journey and encourage enjoyment at the same time?

#engaginglearning
#learn
#connect

Idea 11: Integrity matters

Implement strategies to ensure you keep your promises to students.

The word integrity is defined as 'the quality of being honest and having strong moral principles'. It's a word that holds much importance when thinking about educating young people. Think of our day-to-day interactions in school. We've all been there. You're on your third cup of coffee and you've just devoured another leftover chocolate from the unwanted Christmas gifts lying around in the office. The caffeine and sugar are getting you through a tough day. A student makes a request. You say you will sort out the request and then it completely slips your mind. It's understandable. Teaching is often one of those plate-spinning roles where you simply can't think about everything all at once, even though you try your best, right? Think about some of these phrases: 'Sure, I'll have it for you first thing tomorrow'; 'Yep, come and see me at breaktime,' and 'I promise to do it when I get home.' Sure enough, the day arrives and you haven't fulfilled your intentions. However unintentional the broken promise might be, it is important to try and avoid it in the future. If students begin to learn that you don't mean what you say, things can become strained.

If you say you are going to do something, make sure you do it

I have fallen prey to this particular maxim in the past. For me, it's usually a promise to get additional work done for someone and when they arrive I simply haven't done it and I feel awful. The way I avoid this happening now is to give myself plenty of time to adhere to the request. That way, I am less stressed and when the student comes along, I am ready for them. Likewise, if you have promised to make a phone call home to parents, you must do it. Students feel wronged when you've told them you'll make a positive call home and you don't get round to it, and it is potentially damaging to the teacher–student relationship. A good way to ensure this happens is to have a time set aside each week dedicated purely for phone calls. If students know when this day is, that helps too.

#integritymatters
#sayitdoit

Idea 12: Role model ready

We must model the behaviour we wish to see in our students.

We are role models. Students look to us for support, advice and guidance in all aspects of life. If we aren't modelling the behaviour we wish to see in our students, then do we really have any integrity when we teach them about being healthy in life and staying organised? I'm not saying we all have to be righteous human beings for the entire time we are teachers, but I think there are some small ideas to keep in mind when dealing with young adults.

- **Exercise:** I constantly talk to my students about the power of exercise. I discuss the exercise I complete each week and attach its importance to my mental health. I also often walk around the playground at break or lunchtime. This not only helps my own wellbeing, but demonstrates the positive behaviour I wish to see in my students. They need to see the connections between mind and body.
- **Diet:** I also avoid drinking too many cups of tea or coffee when students are around and avoid eating too many sugary snacks in front of them. That's not to say there aren't sweet treats every now and then, but it's definitely not a daily or even weekly occurrence.
- **Environment care:** Another quick win is to pick up rubbish and put it in the bin whenever you pass some. Do you recycle paper in your classroom or does it go straight in the bin? Are you drinking from a sustainable container or are you buying single-use plastic?
- **Communication around the school:** Are you discussing other staff members within earshot of students? Can they hear you? Are you saying productive and supportive things or the contrary? Young people are curious sponges who love gossip! They need to know the adults in charge are working together for their school community, so work as a team in public and solve potential issues in private.

None of us are perfect, least of all me, but if we are mindful our behaviours will have a positive effect on those we teach.

> **Next steps**
> Consider your own approach to the things above. Is there one thing you could improve this week?

#rolemodel
#connect

Idea 13: Keeping it calm

Controlling the noise level in your classroom supports student wellbeing and learning.

As teachers it is our responsibility to ensure students feel comfortable enough to learn in our classrooms. One of the most important things you can do for students in your lessons is to keep the learning environment calm and controlled. Some students can find it incredibly stressful if the noise level in your classroom is too high. It can hamper their learning as well as distress them.

One way to monitor this is by using the Bouncy Balls app (BouncyBalls.org). This app was shared by Martin Burrett (@ICTmagic) at a TeachMeet of mine. It allows users to monitor the level of noise in a room by showing balls bouncing. The higher they bounce, the louder the noise level in the room. You can change the balls to eyeballs, emojis and bubbles. If students need a visual tool to help them understand the importance of moderating their voice, this could work as long as they aren't easily distracted!

Often, you may wish for the students to be working hard on their own. I insist on silence whenever students are doing independent work. If you want students to be silent you must ask them to be silent, not quiet. By asking the students to be quiet, you are suggesting that they can make some level of noise, which sends the wrong instruction. In every lesson, I have at least 25 minutes of silence and often longer. There is no need for students to be talking as the activities you will have delivered prior to this have led to them being able to work independently. You will find that students are able to concentrate far better in this kind of learning environment and feel much calmer as a result. They also get much more work done and therefore, they make quicker progress. Don't be afraid to insist on silence.

Next steps
If you struggle to instil silence in your classroom, line the class up outside again and ask them to enter quietly. Repeat this until they understand your expectations.

#learn
#keepcalmteacher

Idea 14: Organised action

Organising and setting yourself up for the day or week reduces feelings of panic and stress.

We all know that feeling of agitation that manifests when you realise you're going to be late for work if you don't get a move on. Your alarm was set to snooze just one too many times and you now find yourself running out the front door, arms full of bags, books and board pens, and a half-eaten piece of toast dangling precariously from your mouth. Luckily for us, this doesn't happen too often, but for students, this can be a daily reality. Without being taught effective time-keeping and organisational skills, they can and do flounder. As teachers, it is our responsibility to pass on the knowledge that will allow students to enter the classroom in a calm and collected manner instead of a flustered, ill-equipped mess. Below are some top tips to share with students.

- Ask them to empty their school bag every weekend and repack it ready for the following week. They may just find that assessment they were looking for in the murky depths of their bag.
- Ensure they review their timetable on a Sunday. They need to know which subjects they are being taught and when any home learning is due.
- Each evening, before they go to bed, ask them to pack their school bag. Advise them to take only the books needed for that day. I've seen too many Year 7s keel over under the weight of their school bags!
- Remind them to have a pre-prepared packed lunch ready. This will avoid them snacking on junk food and will help them to avoid spending money. If they eat school dinners, ask them to check they have enough money on their payment card (most schools operate a cashless payment system now) or if they have enough money to pay for it.
- Remind them to get their uniform washed every week and to set it out in their room every night. That way they will not be in a rush searching for their tie when they should already be on the school bus.
- Advise them to set their alarm slightly earlier than they need to if they are prolific snoozers!
- If they take public transport to school, advise them to plan to catch an earlier bus. That way, if they are running late, they have given themselves some leeway.

#letsgetorganised

Chapter 2

Recognition mission

Recognising the efforts of others is an important life skill that should be both modelled and practised in schools.

We all know how easy it is to get bogged down with the daily grind of being a busy frontline teacher. There are days when you may not speak to anyone at all. And there are days when you crave some kind of interaction with others. Imagine if you were a student feeling like this. No one to talk to. No one to notice you. You're basically invisible. It's a pretty grim thought, isn't it? No child should ever feel this way at school and equally, they should also be taught how to show recognition and gratitude to others. This chapter is full of ideas to help with this aim.

In the chapter you will find simple yet effective ideas that focus on both recognising student effort and encouraging them to show gratitude to others. You will find small tips about the power of a simple thank you; plenty of ideas about how to effectively use praise; 'student shout out' ideas; tricks to implement effective recognition in lessons; and ideas you can use to recognise students in form time. It's not an exhaustive list and it would obviously not be wise to try them all at once, but why not give one or two ideas a trial in your classroom? I'd love to know how you get on.

Idea 15: The power of thank you

A small thank you really does go a long way.

The power of a thank you has long been known to those who understand the importance of kindness. We are all taught to say thank you from a very young age. Research has shown that it really does go a long way to supporting the wellbeing of others, not to mention ourselves. Saying thank you encourages the practice of gratitude. When we consider things we are thankful for and make an effort to thank people in the process, both parties feel good about themselves. It's a win-win situation. It is the basis for building long-lasting, effective relationships, which are essential in society. One study by researchers at SWPS University of Social Sciences and Humanities in Poland found that practising gratitude improved wellbeing and promoted a greater sense of social support. What better information to share with students about the importance of a thank you?

There are many ways in which students can be encouraged to say thank you to others. Here are just a few:

- **Thank three:** At the end of every week, hand your form groups three thank you slips. Ask them to write down the names of three people who have helped or supported them in some way that week. These can be delivered to the relevant form group or placed in a teacher's post tray. I started this with my Year 7 form recently and they love it! It's also heart-warming to hear from the people they have thanked about how it has brightened their day.
- **Form thanks:** In form time ask a member of the group who they are thankful for in the form and why. This strengthens the bond between your tutees and encourages them to be more social with each other. It's also a great way to get to know your form as you will begin to notice patterns and friendships emerging.
- **Postcards:** Practise what you preach by sending home postcards of thanks to students who have worked particularly hard. As a department, we do this at the end of every half term. Our students love receiving them in the post and it supports positive relationships with their parents too.

- **Parents' evening:** If a student is truly deserving of this, begin a parent meeting by thanking them for raising such a wonderful student. I've lost count of the amount of times this has caught parents by surprise. They are genuinely delighted to receive such positive praise about their offspring and it's a great way to start off a meeting. This also strengthens your relationship with the student in question.
- **Lesson contributions:** Always, always, always thank students for their contributions during lessons. Do you remember when you were that small and were asked to speak in class? It's pretty nerve-wracking for some. By thanking them for their contribution, you are showing gratitude, validating their response and further encouraging them to speak out again in the future. Thank them individually as they leave your room too, even if they didn't speak out publicly. They still came in and (hopefully) tried their best to succeed.
- **Positive behaviour points system:** Most schools have a points-based merit system to recognise the efforts of students on a daily basis. If your school has one, use it to thank students for their effort. One of the best times of my day is when, as a tutor, I get to read out all the positive comments made by teachers about the students in my form. It's a great way to pass on thanks and students love listening to what their teachers had to say about them. It also ends their day on a high. They feel valued for their efforts and their tutor is happy and proud too. If your school doesn't have this system, use the praise system they have in place to reward your students.
- **Thank you cards:** I keep a box of these on my desk. Throughout the year, for whatever reason, some students might need to feel appreciated. If that is the case, I slip a little thank you card in their exercise book. It usually contains a personal message of thanks for something they've done. These cards are particularly effective when the student in question is struggling to see the best in themselves.

These are just a few ideas that I use to both encourage young people to be grateful and also model gratitude myself. Give them a go and see what happens. I'd love to hear what you think.

> **Next steps**
> At the start of the next academic year, why not map out your approach to including more gratitude ideas in your lessons? Choose perhaps two or three to begin with and see if you notice the difference at the end of the first term. You could even take surveys at the beginning and end of the term to measure progress.

#powerofthankyou
#gratitude

Idea 16: Praise, praise, praise

Praise raises students' self-esteem and confidence.

It's well known by teachers across the world that students respond positively to praise, but it can be all too easy to forget when you're trying to make your way through a busy week. Often, the effort put in by some students deserves some special recognition, and what better way to do it than by praising them for their hard work?

There are many benefits to praising students, aside from encouraging motivation to make better progress. Their confidence builds as we reward their effort, which in turn improves their wellbeing. Making contact with parents to praise students has the added benefit of improving communication between the school and home, which helps raise attainment.

Remember praise should only be offered when a student has worked for it. If you sprinkle it all over the place like confetti without a thought about why, it can prove ineffective. Praise for effort, nothing else.

How can you begin?

Below are just some of the ways in which you can recognise student effort and success:

- **Postcards or phone calls home:** These work really well as the students often receive double praise from both their teacher and their parents or carers. Set aside time each week or half term to call home to ensure regular contact and praise are received.
- **House points, positive points or credits:** Whatever you call them, award them generously for effort. One school I worked at had someone who took the lead in this area. I would receive a weekly email informing me whether I had hit my award target or not. It also included a breakdown of which classes I had given the awards to. This helped me realise I wasn't always awarding the points evenly and was perhaps showing some unconscious bias towards certain groups or students.
- **Exercise book recognition:** If you want students to have high standards in their exercise books, reward them for doing so. I share

a slide each week that credits anyone whose exercise book is of a high standard with work completed. I also leave little notes of extra recognition in exercise books where students have written something particularly good. They get very excited when they see these! Sticky note praise also works well here. As we no longer mark books in my current school, it can be a nice surprise for students to receive a little sticky note on the front of their book recognising their effort (see Idea 21: Secret stickies on page 29).

- **Subject awards:** These are handed out at the end of every term and should be awarded to those who have worked exceptionally hard in different subject areas. I use the 'I heard a Wispa' award too. Each week, staff in my department nominate a student who has worked well and put in consistent effort and they are awarded with a certificate and a Wispa® chocolate bar. These are delivered on Friday by the English leaders. This idea was taken from my previous school, Long Field Academy.

- **Assembly awards:** Why not nominate and recognise student effort in whole-school assemblies? The more you create an environment that recognises effort as a success, the more students will begin to believe they can achieve.

- **Choice:** Offer students a choice in your lesson as a reward for excellent classwork. It could be that they get to choose where they sit or which homework task they would like to do. Students love choice and it gives them some ownership of their learning.

- **Prizes:** There is much debate about the use of prizes as a reward or outcome of praise, but if exercised well, this can be a great way to show students you appreciate their hard work. For example, consider the choice of prize you are offering. At my school, students are awarded book vouchers to spend in the local store. This encourages them to read as well as to continue to work hard.

Next steps

As a school, you could consider offering reward trips for those who consistently put in their best effort. This obviously shouldn't be the only opportunity for students to go on a trip, but it will encourage them to work hard, as they will want to go! At my school, reward trips take place each term. Those with exemplary behaviour records, who put in consistent effort every day, are invited to take part in trips such as ice skating, bowling and climbing. Students enjoy the trips so much and it certainly reinforces positive learning behaviours once back at school.

#praisepraisepraise
#notice
#praiseforeffort

Idea 17: Poetry power

Personalising a message to your students shows them how much you care.

For the past four years, I have been writing a poem for my class at the end of a school year to say goodbye to my Year 11 leavers. It started off as something small and now they have grown into full-form poems, often in iambic pentameter with rhyming couplets! This year, I decided to analyse the poem, providing students with both these notes and a copy of the poem, which added even more meaning to the gesture. Students absolutely love receiving them. Dale Carnegie, author of *How to Win Friends and Influence People*, says, 'A person's name is, to that person, the sweetest and most important sound in any language.' Using a student's name in such a special way makes them feel valued and noticed.

I'm sure you may be thinking, 'I can't write poetry. You must be mad!' But the thing is, you don't have to be an expert in writing to begin your poetry journey. Here are some simple styles of poetry you can replicate:

- **Acrostic poems:** A poem in which the first letter of each line spells out a word, message or the alphabet. These are simple and fun to try. Give it a go!
- **Limerick:** A humorous poem consisting of five lines. The first, second, and fifth lines must have seven to ten syllables while rhyming and having the same rhythm. The third and fourth lines only have to have five to seven syllables, and have to rhyme with each other and have the same rhythm. These are super fun and often leave the class in stitches!
- **Sonnet:** A poem of 14 lines using any of a number of formal rhyme schemes and typically having ten syllables per line. Okay, so this one might be a little more difficult to master, but who's to say it has to fit perfectly to the form? It can be as creative as you like.

Next steps

If you're really struggling with the poem, why not try a short story or tale instead? That way you could include everything you want to about the students in your class without the added worry of trying to make it rhyme or fit a particular form.

#poetrypower
#personaltouch

Idea 18: Student shout out

Encouraging students to recognise each other's efforts improves relationships.

As educators, it's important that we encourage students to recognise and praise the efforts of their peers by learning the art of gratitude. This encourages them to effectively build positive relationships within the school community. There is a plethora of reasons as to why practising gratitude is important. Firstly, showing appreciation for others encourages them to seek an ongoing relationship with the person showing gratitude. It also improves the physical and psychological health of the person showing gratitude. In a study conducted at the University of Kentucky, researchers found that showing gratitude increases empathy and reduces aggression. It also improves the self-esteem of the person offering gratitude. It's not hard to see why encouraging our students to show more gratitude is a worthy task!

Here is a way in which this can be done. Create 'student shout out' nomination boxes for each year group and place them somewhere central in the school. Each week, ask students to nominate someone who has gone the extra mile for them. It can be for any reason, such as helping another student with some homework; walking to school with a new student; or being a listening ear when they needed someone to talk to. Have form representatives collect the nomination slips and drop them into the boxes each week. When the weekly assembly arrives, a name can be drawn and a prize given. This ensures that the entire student body is not only encouraged to nominate, but also shares the moment of the winner's joy. It instantly creates a celebratory feel to the assembly. If you want to go one step further and really spread the gratitude love, you can ask school council leaders to deliver the remaining nominations to the students named. That way everyone gets to find out they were nominated and it increases the feeling of kindness and support across the school community.

Next steps
Why not have an end-of-term whole-school nomination system too? All students can nominate someone who they feel is really deserving of an extra special award. Make it even more celebratory by naming the winner across the school and informing parents.

#studentshoutout
#notice

Idea 19: Secret wellbeing challenge

Encouraging students to actively show appreciation supports their own wellbeing.

This year, I have been encouraging students in my form to be more community-focused. One of the ways in which this has been executed is through the 'Secret wellbeing challenge'. The idea is simple: every week students take part in a secret challenge that involves doing something nice for another student or staff member. If a staff member or student reports back on what they have done, the student mentioned wins a positive behaviour point.

It works for a number of reasons. Firstly, the students love the idea that it is a secret. They are told if they tell teachers what they are doing, it will spoil the challenge and they won't be awarded their point. Secondly, it genuinely teaches them how to be more altruistic and they feel good about completing the tasks. Thirdly, the form gain a reputation around the school as a truly lovely form. Finally, they are spreading a little bit of joy everywhere they go! Teachers and other students love being cared for by each other. It makes for a much happier environment all round. This idea works best in the second half of the autumn term when the days are dark and the pressure of school life mounts.

Here are some of the challenges that your students could take part in, split over an eight-week half term.

Week 1: Hold the door open for anyone you see. Yes, this should be a given, but allowing students to solely focus on the act instils kindness explicitly. Oh, and it spreads like wildfire too. A simple act like this can go a long way when 30 plus students are deliberately doing it across the school.

Week 2: Compliment week. Find someone deserving and compliment them. It can be a teacher complimented on their lesson, assembly, or something they did that made the student's day a little more exciting. It can be a friend they really admire or even their parents! Remind students that it has to be genuine. This idea really works because other staff members often feed back to you as the form tutor. When you tell the students what other staff have said about them, they can see it really works.

Week 3: Gratitude week. Give each student three gratitude slips. Ask them to hand them out across the week to people who they feel grateful to have in their lives. There should be space on the card for them to write a reason why they are grateful for their chosen person. This really encourages them to focus on the positive aspects of their life.

Week 4: 'How do you do?' week. Encourage students to ask each other and the entire school community how they are. By asking them to be a listening ear, it develops their empathy levels and also makes for a far more supportive school environment.

Week 5: Favour week. Ask students to offer help to their teachers. Examples include: can I clean your board? Shall I hand the books out? These small things make a big difference in the lives of busy teachers and it encourages students to be aware of the needs of others.

Week 6: Postcards of Kindness week. Encourage students to get involved in the Postcards of Kindness scheme (see Idea 70: Postcards of Kindness on page 121). Reward students who get involved.

Week 7: Thank a teaching assistant (TA) week. TAs spend hours supporting our students and deserve a little recognition from them too. Offer your students two thank you slips. Ask them to give them to a TA who makes their life better. It will really make their day.

Week 8: Christmas card week. Offer students five Christmas cards each and ask them to send them to people who they think deserve a little Christmas pick-me-up. Instruct them to choose people who aren't their close friends to spread Christmas cheer.

At the end of the half term, ask students to reflect on how the challenge made them feel. You can share all of the wonderful things people have said about the students. This could be collated as you go through the challenges each week. I make a short video backed by some suitable music to share the wonderful messages. It really ends what can be a difficult term for both staff and students on a high.

#secretwellbeing
#notice
#volunteer

Next steps

Why not roll this out across a whole year group or even the entire school? All staff would need to be on board in keeping the 'secret', instructing their form not to discuss their challenge, but it is a wonderful idea to improve day-to-day feeling.

Idea 20: Feel Good Friday

Fridays should be a time to celebrate success and reflect on the week.

In my form, we use Fridays as a way of reviewing the week. It ensures that the students go home that week feeling accomplished and valued by the school community. We all know the benefits of recognising student achievement: it builds self-esteem and confidence; it encourages future positive behaviour; it develops a sense of community; and it shows young people that their efforts do not go unrecognised.

So, how can you make Fridays feel good for your students?

- **Achievement certificates:** Keep hold of any certificates that are handed over to you by other staff members during the week and present these to the students in form time in front of their peers. Better still, make your own certificates of achievement and share these too!
- **Sharing is caring:** Ask students to share their favourite thing about the week and explain why. This encourages them to focus on the positive things that have taken place.
- **Music fall out:** I usually ask the student who received the most positive points in a week (see Idea 16: Praise, praise, praise on page 22) to choose a song that they can listen to as they leave the classroom. They love getting to choose and they leave with a real buzz about them. This also helps the students to learn more about each other.
- **Small treats:** This isn't everyone's cup of tea, but every now and then I might reward my form with a small treat. Some weeks the students can simply be above and beyond awesome and it is nice to recognise that with something extra special.

This is not an exhaustive list, but you get the idea. The key to this idea is to make sure that the students in your care leave on Friday feeling good about themselves and good about the school. That way, they'll be excited to come back again on Monday.

> **Next steps**
> Why not review the way Friday form is completed across the school? Wouldn't it be great if all students left on a Friday in a positive mood?

#feelgoodfriday
#connect
#notice

Idea 21: Secret stickies

Leaving small notes of recognition in student books ensures their efforts are recognised and makes them feel valued.

An idea that I regularly use in my classroom is 'secret stickies'. Before I delve into the actual process of this idea, I think it's important to understand why it is so successful. Allow me to ask a few questions: are you aware of the effort that every single child makes in your classroom every day? Do you notice the quieter students who rarely get things wrong, yet always do their work in a calm and unassuming manner? It can be all too easy to forget about these students when your energy and attention in class is directed to some raucous characters, or students who always want to contribute more. In my classroom, I ensure that everyone contributes through questioning, but aside from this technique the same students will always choose to remain silent, yet perform highly in written assessments. So how can we ensure that those quieter students are always recognised for their hard work and consistent effort? The answer: secret stickies.

How it works

Secret stickies are an incredibly simple idea. First things first, make sure you have a bunch of sticky notes at all times. Secondly, whenever you are looking through student books, leave secret stickies with messages of praise on them in their books. My heart will always be warmed by the shy smiles that occur when students are given their books and they open them to find the notes. This is often the type of praise these students need and enjoy. A quiet acknowledgement that you have recognised their efforts and appreciate their presence in your lessons. It is cost-effective, takes very little time to administer and the benefits are clear to see.

> **Next steps**
> Why not start small? Wander through your class with the stickies and place a message of praise on a student's book. You'll be slapping those colourful little notes everywhere once you see the impact it can have.

#secretstickies
#praise

Idea 22: Tutor time care

Tutor time is the perfect opportunity to nurture young people and show them that you care.

Tutors are responsible for the pastoral welfare of the young people in their care. It is vital that our tutees feel like they are cared for and that they feel a sense of belonging within their tutor group. Schools can be very lonely places for young people. Tutors have a responsibility to ensure they don't feel so isolated. Most schools have a regular timetable of activities for tutor time, but that doesn't mean you can't include some of your own personal touches to show the young people in your form that you care and to promote gratitude in all its forms.

Here are some ideas that support this aim.

- **Spiritual reflection:** Once a week, discuss and consider a theme: compassion, gratitude, empathy, injustice, and so on. By starting or ending the day thinking about others, you are encouraging young people to care about the community.
- **Mindfulness colouring books:** These are great for students who just need to take some time out. They promote a calm perspective.
- **Achievement jar:** Every student writes down something they are proud of and places it in the jar. This promotes positive feeling amongst the group and feelings of gratitude.
- **Birthdays:** It's a great idea to celebrate birthdays of members in your form. It makes them feel recognised and special. Why not buy each tutee a cupcake and a card from the class to really celebrate?
- **Wellbeing programme:** A fully designed activity where different topics are looked at each week. Topics such as self-esteem, body image, LGBTQ, equality, and so on could be explored. This is quite a big task so it would be a good idea to discuss it with your PSHE lead so that it can be a whole-school strategy.
- **Creative reflection journals:** Encourage students to reflect on their week with these in any way they wish.
- **Retrieval practice:** See Idea 42 for more about this. This could be about the messages of the weekly assembly, or even about developing the literacy and numeracy of tutees.
- **Silent reading:** This is a fantastic way to support the wellbeing of young people and teaches them the importance of reading.

- **Class read:** My form absolutely loves the class read. We do this once a week and they are so excited to find out what will happen next in the plot. This can be done either by reading to them, which I feel works best, or you can encourage students to read some too.
- **Shared gratitude:** Ask students to say something they like and appreciate about someone else in the class.
- **Register games:** This can be about anything you like. You can ask them questions such as, 'If you could be anywhere in the world right now, where would you be and why?' These types of questions ensure that you really get to know your tutees and, in turn, they feel that you are genuinely taking an interest in their lives.
- **Just dance:** Why not put on a song (there are plenty available on YouTube) and encourage students to have a good old shake around? This really invigorates the start of their day.
- **Desert island discs:** Have students pick three songs that are special to them and explain why to the rest of the class. They also have to pick one book they couldn't live without and explain why.
- **Positive praise time:** Every day, share the positive points (see Idea 16) your form received. This is something they really enjoy as they feel like their day has gone well if they have received these. It ends each day on a high. It is also a good idea to keep a record of who has achieved the most points each week and throughout the year too. Your registration system will be able to help you with this, so do seek advice about how to find this data.
- **Tutor rooms roles:** Tutees can take it in turns to keep the classroom tidy. Jobs could include: watering the plants, tidying the book shelf, cleaning the board or making sure displays are neat. Students love contributing to the classroom tidiness as they see it as their space.
- **Mindfulness activities:** There are heaps of these available online. One example is to ask students to count on their fingers ten things they are grateful for in their life. This encourages feelings of gratitude. Try looking at the Mindfulness in Schools Project website for ideas: www.mindfulnessinschools.org.

Next steps

There are plenty of resources online that you could use to develop activities in form time. The Hectic Teacher (@HecticTeacher) has a tutor challenge booklet as well as a weekly reflections resource, which you can find on her website: hecticteachersite.wordpress.com/catageory/tutor. Why not share these with all the form tutors in school so you have a consistent approach?

#tutortimecare
#gratitude
#connect

Idea 23: Visualiser vision

Using a visualiser to recognise student work builds pride and motivation amongst them.

If you do not yet own a visualiser in your classroom, I urge you to acquire one as soon as you can. Essentially, a visualiser is a document camera that, when connected to your computer and screen, allows you to see anything that is placed under its lens. They are incredibly useful for many reasons, but most importantly for this book's chapter on recognition, you can use them to showcase excellent examples of students' written work the moment they have finished the task.

How to get started

Firstly, ask your department lead if they can budget for a visualiser for your classroom. If they are unsure of the impact they have, share this blog: www.tes.com/news/ditch-powerpoint-visualiser-now-rules.

Secondly, make a plan about how you are going to introduce this new tool to your classroom and students. Initially, it may cause some trepidation amongst students and the last thing you want is unhappy or nervous learners. Start by explaining its benefits to their learning and perhaps use it to annotate or live model some writing before you place a student's work under the lens. Warn them that next lesson you intend to use it to showcase their excellent work so that they are aware of your expectations. That way, there will be no surprises in the next lesson.

Next lesson, as they are writing, walk around and check whose work is evidencing the skills you have been learning together. Subtly, ask them if they wouldn't mind sharing. Try to choose a more confident character initially and build up to ensuring all students are being approached. Once the work is on screen, work through it annotating and explaining why it is successful. Students should be given the chance to articulate this too. It's a fantastic way to show recognition of a job well done!

Next steps

Why not have students who are secure in knowledge and skill live model instead of you? This really builds confidence and encourages others to be successful.

#visualiservision
#recognition

Idea 24: Gratitude letters

Encourage students to show gratitude to those who have been supportive.

A great way to role model positive recognition behaviours with young people is to practise writing gratitude letters with them. There are many benefits to this type of activity. For example, it enhances empathy, builds effective relationships, improves self-esteem and increases mental strength.

Here's how it can be done:

- Have students think about the last few weeks of their lives. Ask them to jot down any notes about what people have done for them. Offer them examples to get them going. Things like: my mum has dropped me off at school every day or my dad allowed me to go to a friend's birthday party last week.
- Next, ask them to choose someone from their notes who they think deserves some recognition for their time and effort towards them and ask them to write down anything else they can think of that their chosen person has done recently. This information will form the basis of their letter.
- Then, ask them to write a letter to their chosen person thanking them for something they are grateful for. You may need to have a model letter and letter-writing template ready to share with the class as some can be reluctant to begin if they don't know how or what to write.
- This idea needs time and careful planning, but once the letters are written, they can be sent home through the post. What a lovely surprise for the students' families and friends!

#gratitudeletters
#showyoucare
#notice

Next steps
Why not set this up as a termly event? It can be something that the class do as a collective activity at the end of each term. It's a great way to encourage students to focus on the positives in their life as they go off to have another break from learning, and it's a nice regular treat for the parents too!

Idea 25: Parent power

Parents and guardians play an important role in the recognition of student success.

It has been long known to educators that parents are enormously important when it comes to the successful progression of students. Every time a survey is conducted at my current school on praise and reward, the top two choices of reward selected by students are postcards and phone calls home. They absolutely love it. Some even go so far as to request a call after each lesson or week if they have 'been good.' The power of effective relationships between teachers and parents is clear to see. Here are some ideas about how to make connections with parents so that students are better supported and recognised for their success.

- Hold a 'getting to know you' parent event early on in the first term for the new Year 7 cohort. This is the perfect opportunity to get to know each student's parents or guardians. Here, you will soon realise who is supportive of the school and who you need to work harder with in order to gain support. Spend time showing parents and guardians that you know their child. Praise them and discuss how they are settling in.
- Set up regular contact with parents if you need to give extra support to more vulnerable students. A close connection will ensure you can fully support their child and work together to develop them.
- Know the best method of contacting each student's parents. Some parents prefer email and some prefer a call.
- Use the best way of contact to praise each student when you think they deserve it. This has such a positive impact on the student's motivation and willingness to succeed.
- Ensure parents and guardians have access to the behaviour record that your school uses. Many parents tend not to know about the systems a school has in place and so might unintentionally miss important messages of praise that their child has received.
- Invite parents along on school trips and charity events to forge even stronger links. Students are much more likely to become involved in such events if their parents are engaged too.

#parentpower
#connect

Idea 26: Wider recognition

Sharing the success of students with a wider audience can help to boost their feelings of self-worth and value.

Everyone loves recognition of a job well done and that isn't any different for our students. A great way to show how much you value their work is to share it on a much wider platform than on the walls of the corridors in your own school. Equally, you may wish to share the much more general success of students in your school regionally or nationally. There are various ways in which this can be done. Here are some below.

- **Parents' evenings or open evenings:** Having student work on display during these events is a great way to show students how much you care about their efforts. I love it when a child comes to an event like this and they instantly take their parent or guardian over to their work. They clearly feel a sense of pride in their achievements and that's what it's all about!
- **Social media:** Lots of schools use their social media platforms to share student work. It's a fantastic way to reach parents and the local community as well as boost students' confidence.
- **Awards:** Nominating students for regional or national awards is a fantastic way to promote them and boost their wellbeing at the same time. An example is the Jack Petchey Awards, which can be found here: www.jackpetcheyfoundation.org.uk/opportunities/jack-petcheys-community-nominations.
- **Competitions:** There are plenty of competitions run nationally for students to enter. A simple subject-specific search online will reveal a wealth of opportunities. What better boost to a child's wellbeing than to know their work is good enough for national competition entry and could even be a winner! Every year at my school, we have student work published in short story anthologies and it's a joy to celebrate the launch events with them and their parents.
- **Newsletter:** Why not showcase exemplary student work through a weekly newsletter to parents? Imagine the joy it will bring to a young person to see their work shared with the entire school community.

#nationalsuccess
#connect

Idea 27: The little things

Taking the time to show students you care really does have a big impact on their wellbeing.

I don't think there's anything more powerful than the day-to-day notice we take of the young people in our care. I've certainly noticed over the ten years I have been teaching that I have greater relationships with students if I take the time to notice them individually. Notice their little quirks and personality traits. Notice their stories about family. Notice their wins for the school's sports teams and so on. So, why is it so important? The simple answer is that everyone loves to feel valued. They love to feel important and part of something much bigger. It is the day-to-day interactions that we have with students that can often have the biggest impact on their wellbeing. They gain a sense of belonging they might not get if you otherwise did not make the effort. So, consider how you do this in your school.

What can you do to ensure students are recognised?

Here are some ideas you could try.

- **Names:** Learn student names and use them at all times. Our name is one of the most precious things to each and every one of us. It is why we all love personalised gifts. The quicker you learn the names of your students, the easier building relationships with them will be and the sooner they will feel valued. Use register games, name tags and seating plans to ensure you learn names as quickly as you can.
- **Congratulate them:** If they have taken part in something school-related, such as the school show or a sporting event, make sure they know that you know about it by congratulating them. It takes less than a minute to do this in passing in the corridor or in your lesson and the smiles you receive in return are worth it.
- **Make time:** This can be a tricky one, but try to make time for students if they are making the effort to come and talk to you or if they invite you along to something school-related. It shows that they value you and it's something you should be proud of. At my school, the football team always want me to watch them play after school. I make it my mission to watch at least half of the match. They are full

of pride when I go along to watch and it's great to see them outside of the classroom context.

- **Know them:** Get to know them by asking questions. What are they doing over the weekend? How do they plan to spend their summer? What's their favourite hobby? These little snippets of information can be used to build strong relationships with students who may not have such effective ties with adults elsewhere in their lives. It makes all the difference to them that you care.

- **Greet them:** Greet them into your classroom, of course, but more importantly, greet them in the corridor. Smile, say hello, ask them how their day is going. When you are on duty, chat to them or play table tennis with them. It is these small events that can make a student's day. Schools should be filled with warm, kind moments like these. Try this with all students, not just the ones you teach. This is beneficial when you come to dealing with students in situations that may be less positive. The more you get to know each student, the greater the relationships within the school will be.

- **Challenge them:** Quiz them at all times. I often wander through the corridor and ask students to list five newly learnt Tier 2 words or three facts they have learnt that day. They like the challenge that I have set and feel proud that they can show off their learning. Students, however much they might deny it, love to learn. It's also nice to let teachers know if they have given you words or facts they have learnt in their subject. This has the effect of further strengthening relationships between that student and the named teacher.

Next steps

Make a plan to talk to every student you pass in the corridor this week. It doesn't have to be for long. A simple 'Hello, how are you?' will suffice. You'll be surprised at the reaction you get.

#littlethingsbigdifference
#notice

Chapter 3

Soothe away stress

The ability to learn is significantly reduced when stress levels are high, so it's important to recognise this and offer support to students who are in need.

Just as we teachers feel bogged down and under pressure from often unmanageable workloads, so do our students often feel overwhelmed and stressed about their own learning challenges. As educators, we should be aware of the pressure points for the young people we serve and be ready and on hand to offer advice and guidance when things are getting a little bit too much for them. This is particularly important during exam season.

This chapter is full of ideas about how to help students de-stress. It is important to note that these ideas are to support general emotional needs your students may be experiencing and they do not in any way act as a substitute for the professional support some students may require. You will find tried and tested methods such as reading to relax, running to de-stress and music to unwind. There are also more practical suggestions, such as keeping a reflective journal and a list of NHS-recommended apps to ensure students who are in need of support can access it at home too. Sharing these ideas with your students could make all the difference to their general wellbeing.

Idea 28: Reading release

Reading allows young people to escape the pressures of their world for a short time.

There are many benefits that come with reading for pleasure and as educators we should all be encouraging students to read as much as they can. Some of the wellbeing benefits of reading for pleasure are:

- **Reading makes you more empathetic.** Literary fiction, in particular, affords young readers the opportunity to relate to others through the creation of detailed and interesting characters. It helps them to understand other people's emotions.
- **Reading helps you to relax.** A study undertaken in 2009 by Sussex University researchers showed that reading may reduce stress by as much as 68 per cent. In fact, reading for just six minutes slows down the heart rate and eases tension in muscles.
- **Reading improves sleep patterns.** Encouraging students to read before bed will calm their mind and prepare their body for sleep. This is especially true for actual books, rather than e-books.
- **Reading improves concentration.** In order to read, students need to sit quietly. Practising this improves concentration.

Here are some ideas for incorporating student reading into your routines.

- **Tutor time class reads.** Read to the class or have them take turns. Choose a great book and watch their excitement as the plot thickens.
- **Silent reading.** This can be done at the end or beginning of a lesson. Surprisingly, even ten minutes of reading can be enough. Often this can help to calm a class upon entering a classroom too.
- **Ask students what they're reading.** Regular dialogue about reading promotes its importance and encourages students to take it up.
- **Reading list challenge.** Set your class a challenge to read a certain number of books each academic year. Include a range of titles on the list, with a mixture of classics and more contemporary texts.
- **Reading groups.** These come in various forms. Reciprocal reading requires students to take on different roles whilst reading in groups. This is less about reading for pleasure and more about developing reading comprehension. Paired reading is another option.

#readingrelease

Idea 29: Runtastic

Running is so good for the soul and young people should be encouraged to take part in it.

The Daily Mile

The Daily Mile is an initiative set up by the Daily Mile Foundation which encourages students to run, jog or walk a mile every day. Exercising every day reduces the risk of strokes, heart attacks, cardiovascular disease, cancer, Alzheimer's and Parkinson's. Studies have also shown that running every day improves mood, concentration and sleep patterns. Why not see how many staff and students you can get involved in your school?

It takes 15 minutes to complete and no resources or additional staff training are needed. The aim is to get as many students as possible outside in the fresh air and engaging in whatever level of physical activity is suitable for them. Students run in their uniform so there's no time wasted getting changed. It's non-competitive, it's social and students with mobility difficulties can be supported to take part as well.

Running club

Set up a weekly staff and student running club. Aim for the spring term when the warmer days are upon us and go go go! This is usually best done in the morning, but could easily work well after school too. One way to ensure people participate is to offer some fresh fruit and healthy snacks for breakfast. The same benefits as the Daily Mile apply here and it's a great way to boost energy levels and strengthen relationships.

Charity events

Why not take part in a charity event? A previous school I worked at took part in Race for Life by Cancer Research. Not only did hundreds of participants from our school take part but many staff, students and parents turned out to support the runners. The atmosphere on the day was brilliant and it's all for a worthy cause too.

#runtastic

> **Next steps**
> Not quite ready for running? Why not encourage students to walk a mile a day in their lunchtime?

Idea 30: Music medley

Music is a powerful tool for generating the right mood in anyone.

Listen to love songs and it can leave you feeling melancholy. Listen to soft rock and suddenly you're Bonnie Tyler as you wail at the top of your voice in your car on your way to work. Charles Darwin once said, 'If I had my life to live over again, I would have made a rule to read some poetry and listen to some music at least once every week.' There is much scientific research to prove that music is good for your mental health and wellbeing. Here are some of its benefits:

- **Music makes you happier.** When you listen to your favourite songs, dopamine is released into your system, which helps to elicit emotions such as happiness, excitement and joy.
- **Music lowers your stress levels and improves your health.** By listening to your favourite music you reduce the levels of the stress hormone cortisol in your body. This leaves you feeling calmer and ready to take on the tough challenge of learning.
- **Music can help you to sleep better.** A study completed by Semmelweis University, Hungary, found that students who listened to classical music for 45 minutes before they went to bed had better sleep than those who did not.
- **Music reduces depression.** The same study noted above also found that symptoms of depression decreased in the group who were listening to classical music.
- **Music improves learning and memory.** Studies have shown that listening to pleasurable music can help you to recall more information in test conditions.

There are many ways in which you can introduce the benefits of music in schools. Here are some ideas you could try:

- **Music mornings:** Every Wednesday this year as a form tutor I allowed pupils to choose a song they wished to play. This was by far their favourite form time activity. It allowed them to take owner-ship of the activity and ensured they left the room in a good mood ready to take on the day. It's an easy win for student wellbeing. We also listened to songs that were of particular significance to their own cultural backgrounds. This gave them a sense of pride in their heritage and encouraged them to talk more about their own cultural heritage.

- **Music links:** Often at the beginning of lessons I might play a song that is of significance to a new topic we are studying. It might be music that links to a particular character from a book or a time period that you are studying to allow for a greater understanding. Asking students to come up with connections between the topic and the song encourages them to think from the moment they enter the room. It also serves for a calm start to the lesson.

- **Music in assemblies:** Playing music at the start of assemblies ensures students enter the room in the right manner and mood. It also provides a good backing track to any videos you wish to share. As head of house, I have created videos of my entire house's yearly achievements and played this back to them in the final assembly. It makes for powerful viewing if the song chosen is well considered.

- **Music for memory:** Music can be a powerful revision tool if you need to remember content-heavy topics. In English, students have to know 15 anthology poems fairly well. One of the ways past students have done this is by placing the lines of the poems to songs they know well and singing them until they know them off by heart. This works particularly well if the meter of the poem matches the song's rhythm.

- **Creative music:** Why not allow students the freedom to create their own song about a topic you have studied recently? This could be set as a homework task and it allows students to demonstrate understanding. It's also fun to see what they have produced and gives them some ownership of the task.

- **Offer students the chance to play music:** Learning to play an instrument shouldn't be reserved only for those students whose parents can afford it. At my school, we are part of the Music in Secondary Schools Trust, which is a fantastic scheme created by Sir Andrew Lloyd Webber. Every year, students in Year 7 are gifted an instrument and offered free music lessons. We now have a fully formed student orchestra who perform at various points throughout the year and it is wonderful to witness. You can learn more about the scheme here: www.misst.org.uk.

Next steps

Why not have music played through speakers across the school during break times? My first school used to do this and it created a warm and relaxed atmosphere.

#musicmedley
#connect

Idea 31: Breathe

Encouraging young people to practise breathing techniques can help reduce anxiety and stress.

Helping students practise deep breathing can produce many positive benefits. It can relieve stress, relax their mind and body, help them sleep better and improve overall wellbeing. It is also a useful tool to teach students when they are experiencing feelings of anxiety or worry.

Breathing benefits

There are many more benefits to deep breathing. Here are a few.

- **Deep breathing is a natural painkiller.** When you breathe deeply it releases natural endorphins, which are feel-good hormones and natural painkillers.
- **Breathing improves energy levels.** Breathing deeply increases blood flow, which in turn increases the amount of oxygen we receive. The more oxygen we get, the higher our energy levels.
- **Breathing improves posture.** Breathing deeply encourages you to stand correctly. It literally forces your body into a better position. Give it a try! This is great advice to offer when you are encouraging students to run. Good posture supports effective exercise.
- **Breathing improves digestion.** When we breathe deeply more oxygen reaches our entire body, including the digestive system. This makes it work more efficiently. Deep breathing also stimulates the intestines and calms the nervous system, improving digestion.
- **Breathing relaxes the body and mind.** When people are distressed they tend to breathe in a shallow manner, but breathing deeply will reverse the lack of oxygen and allow your mind and body to become calmer.

Breathing techniques

Here are three breathing techniques you could try with your students.

Abdominal breathing exercise
If a student is feeling stressed or anxious, ask them to try abdominal breathing by following these steps.

1. Inhale slowly and deeply through the nose. Ask them to keep their shoulders relaxed as they do this. They should feel their abdomen expanding and their chest moving very little. Tell them to count to five as they breathe in.
2. Exhale slowly through the mouth. As they blow air out remind them to relax their jaw and count to five.
3. Repeat this for several minutes until they feel better.

Breathe focus technique
This uses imagery and/or focus words with the breathing activity.

1. First, ask the student to think of an image or focus word that makes them smile or feel relaxed.
2. Ask them to alternate between normal and deep breaths for a few moments. Ask them to pay attention to how their abdomen expands during the deeper breaths.
3. Ask them to gradually ensure all breaths are deep, focusing on the rise and fall of their abdomen.
4. Once they are fully in deep-breathing mode, ask them to focus on their image or key word and to keep repeating it in their minds.
5. Continue with this method until they have calmed down.

The 4-7-8 breathing technique
This helps to calm down those suffering from anxiety. It requires students to focus on taking in a long, deep breath. This is also used in yoga practices and meditation exercises.

1. Ask the student to empty their lungs of air.
2. Ask them to breathe in quietly and deeply through the nose for four seconds.
3. Next, ask them to hold their breath for seven seconds.
4. Finally, ask them to exhale through the mouth for eight seconds, making a whooshing sound as they do so.
5. Repeat for four cycles or until the student is feeling calm again.

Next steps

Share a breathing app with your students for support when they need it at home. Chill Panda is an NHS-recommended breathing app that helps you learn to relax, manage worries and improve wellbeing. It measures your heart rate and suggests activities to suit your needs, including breathing techniques and light activities to help ease your mind.

#breatheeasy
#notice
#connect

Idea 32: Apps for support

Apps are an easy and efficient way to help students seeking support when they might not feel comfortable talking to someone in person.

One of the benefits of living in a digital age is that there is no shortage of free advice, support and information available. It goes without saying that there is also plenty of information out there that could be potentially damaging to our students. Here are some NHS-recommended apps that students may benefit from.

- **Blueice:** This is an evidence-based app that helps young people manage their emotions and reduce the risk of self-harm. It includes things like a mood diary, stress-relieving techniques as well as automatic routing to emergency numbers if urges to self-harm continue.
- **Catch It:** This app helps young people to manage feelings like anxiety and depression. It teaches ways of looking at problems in a different light and turning negative thoughts into positive ones.
- **Feel Good: Positive mindset:** This app uses audio tracks to help you build confidence, energy and a positive mindset.
- **MeeTwo:** A safe and secure forum for teenagers wanting to discuss any issue affecting their lives. The service is anonymous and advice can be sought from experts or other teenagers who have experienced similar issues, from mental health concerns, to stress, anxiety, and relationship and family problems.
- **Student Health App:** Impressively, this app provides access to more than 900 pages of reliable information all in one place. The content was created by NHS doctors to support university students, but this would also be suitable for A-level students.
- **Thrive:** This app uses games to help prevent and manage stress, anxiety and other related conditions. The app can be used to help you relax before a potentially stressful situation or on a more regular basis to help you live a happier, stress-free life.

> **Next steps**
> Why not deliver a tutor time session discussing the various apps that are freely available for young people so that they know there is support out there should they need it?

#appsupport
#connect

Idea 33: Reflection journal

Reflecting on their day through daily journal writing can help students to organise their thoughts and relieve stress.

Daily school life can be a real challenge for some students, particularly in the run-up to the exam season when students are struggling to organise themselves. A daily reflective journal can help to alleviate some of their stresses and concerns by allowing them to keep track of their learning in a way suited to their own needs. Before I discuss how to incorporate them, let's take a look at the benefits of being reflective learners.

- They are usually motivated to succeed. They know what they are trying to achieve and the purpose of the achievement.
- They usually want to expand their knowledge of a subject or topic. Writing a journal can allow students to organise any unanswered questions they may still have.
- They understand new ideas and concepts by relating them to earlier topics. A reflective journal allows them to make these connections with ease.
- They develop their learning by building on the evaluation of previous ideas. A reflective journal allows them to do this.
- They are aware of their own strengths and weaknesses, and how to approach fixing their weaknesses.
- They can express their feelings through writing.

How to get started

Acquire a class set of notebooks and ask students to spend five to ten minutes each day collecting their thoughts and reflecting on their day. It's important to stress that there is no specific way in which they should write their thoughts down. It is very much their own creation and should stay that way if students are to find it a useful strategy. A great time for students to do this is during afternoon registration. However, it could also provide a calm and collected end to the day or lesson.

> **Next steps**
> Incorporate a reflective activity into a tutor time session each week to get students started on their reflective journey.

#dailyjournal
#notice
#learn

Idea 34: Mindfulness magic

Practising mindfulness techniques keeps students calm and collected.

Teaching students mindful techniques is enormously beneficial throughout their time at secondary school. It reduces stress and anxiety; improves their self-esteem and ability to regulate their emotions; and increases their sense of inner calm. There are many ways to incorporate mindfulness into the school week. Here are some ideas.

Mindful walking

I often use this as a strategy to calm down particularly worked-up young people. Sometimes, the confines of a classroom can fail to restore an anxious or angry student to their calmer state of mind. If this is the case, taking a walk with the student can have the desired effect. It gives them something to do, rather than sit and dwell on the issues that made them upset in the first place. It also releases some of the pent-up energy they are experiencing. The walk need not include talking – sometimes silence is best. Of course, if the student is willing to talk, that's a start. By the time you have returned to the classroom, the student should be calmer and ready to move forward with the day.

Mindful colouring

This activity is great for young people who need to switch off from their emotions and thoughts. Buy some mindful colouring books and offer them to students needing to calm down for ten to 15 minutes. The focus on the colouring enables them to detach from whatever it was that made them worry initially.

Mindful body scan

I learnt about body scanning at a mindfulness course a year ago. It's a great meditation technique that works well with young people. I use this during my group mentor meeting with a bunch of Year 11 girls. It starts the session off in a calm and soothing manner. Ask students to sit in silence with their eyes closed. Starting with the top of the head, instruct students to move their attention all the way through their body until they have reached their toes. Guide them as they do this. Ask them to think about each area as they scan. Ask them to relax their body as they scan. Encourage them to bring mindfulness to each part of their body as they scan. The result is a much calmer individual.

Mindful listening

This is a good activity to use when students are working in pairs. It encourages them to actively listen when someone else is talking and to 'be in the moment'. Once in pairs, give one student a prompt and ask them to talk for two minutes whilst the other student listens. They have the opportunity to question their partner once the talk is over.

Sensory mindfulness

This activity encourages young people to empty their thoughts and focus on something happening in the present as a way of being calm. In a group, have each person say what they notice in terms of the five senses. They can start by saying five things they can see. Then four things they can feel. Three things they can hear. Two things they can smell. Finally, one thing they can taste. Whatever it is, it does the job of forcing them to think about just one thing, rather than have a mind whirring with activity. This can go on for as long as you deem necessary.

Three-step mindfulness

This activity is another way to bring students into a calm state of mind.

- **Step 1:** Step out of autopilot mode and into the present. Ask students to focus on anything going on in the room at that moment.
- **Step 2:** Ask students to focus on their breathing for a couple of minutes. Ask them to think about how their lungs inflate, how their chest rises and falls, and how their belly pushes out. This ensures they are anchored in the present.
- **Step 3:** Expand awareness to the rest of the body and then the immediate environment. Ask students to focus on any feelings they experience from their body. Do they have any aches or tension? If so, encourage them to release this energy. Then ask them to focus on the environment. What do they hear, see, smell, taste and feel?

Students should now feel ready to take on the day.

Next steps
Why not incorporate a weekly mindfulness activity into tutor time sessions or assembly?

#mindfulmagic
#connect
#notice

Idea 35: Routine readiness

Helping students into a routine can support their own organisation skills, prepare them for life and reduce daily stress.

If we want students to be good at managing their workload, then we need to teach them how to set themselves a regular routine when it comes to learning and school life. We all love routine in our lives. I know of some teachers who really struggle with the summer holidays as the routine they are used to during term time is lost. Likewise we are all aware of the difference even the smallest change in routine can have on our students. There's a reason most staff hate non-uniform days! Routines ensure students know what to expect and as such, they are less stressed each day.

What are the benefits of routines?

- **Routines make students more efficient.** If we stick to the same daily routine in school, it reduces the need for them to make daily decisions that could prove stressful. School routines become normal and require less thinking on their part. When there is a change of routine, be sure to explain this to students as the disruption to their day can cause problems.
- **Routines reduce the need for students to plan the day-to-day.** This allows them more time to complete their homework.
- **Routines build good habits in students.** Repeating certain tasks and routines prepares students for the kind of motivation they will need when they eventually enter the world of work; study routines are particularly important for this. Equally, routines are important for any extra-curricular activities in which students wish to excel.
- **Routines encourage students to become more proficient.** They naturally become better at certain things because they are doing them every day. They begin to master the skills they are practising.
- **They help students to prioritise what is important in their life.** Perhaps they know they are particularly stressed before mock exams. Prioritising a mindfulness routine each morning can help them with this.
- **Routines reduce the need for determination and willpower.** The smallest tasks, like brushing your teeth, for example, become routine through daily effort. The same will apply to their learning.

- **Routines reduce procrastination in students.** If they know what to expect every day, they will have less trouble getting started on whatever it is they are doing.
- **Routines build students' momentum coming up to important exams.** If they do a little bit each day, they begin to see the impact it has and by the time exam season arrives, they feel prepared.
- **Routines improve a student's self-confidence.** They give them a feeling of satisfaction when whatever they have been preparing for is successful.
- **Routines reduce stress.** Students' levels of stress are reduced if they are following routines because routines allow them to feel in control of how they approach each day. They can't stop the fact that they will be taking lots of exams, but they can control their approach to them.

With all of these brilliant benefits, it makes sense to ensure our students have a regular routine when they arrive at school. The more consistent the better. It's also important to sweat the small stuff early on. How do students enter your classroom? In my school, they walk in the room in silence, stand behind their chairs and wait to be seated. They always have their planners and equipment out on the desk, as well as their reading books. It is this routine of readiness that prepares them for the day ahead. They know what to expect and what is important.

Ideas to include in your routine

- **Reading:** Regular reading develops students' literacy skills and general love of learning. It's important to build these academic skills into students' weekly routines to prepare them for the next stage of their education.
- **Revision:** Building in revision time and activities in the run-up to the exam season ensures students are able to feel in control of their revision and manage their workload. Equally, allowing them time to build their own revision timetable supports this aim.
- **Equipment check:** Daily equipment checks ensure students understand the importance of being organised and ready to learn.
- **Homework check:** A weekly homework check is also important to keep students focused and reminded of their out-of-school learning responsibilities.

#routinereadiness
#learn

Idea 36: The power of laughter

Laughing is the cure to many negative ailments, not least stress.

Have you ever read the poem *Smile* by Spike Milligan? If not, I recommend you find it online and read it in full before continuing with this idea. I love the sentiment that the poem offers: that smiling is catching. The same goes for laughter. Laughter brings people together. It is one of the most powerful tools we, as educators, can use in our classrooms. You would struggle to find a person in the world who would argue against the positive effects laughter can have upon someone. I've written in Chapter I about the importance of having the right attitude as a teacher in order for your students to feel good in your lessons (see Idea 6: Weather makers, page 8), but this idea is all about how we can use laughter to de-stress our students on a regular basis.

There's science behind why we find it so much fun to laugh together. Here are the facts.

- **Laughter actually relaxes the body.** A good, bottom-of-the-belly, side-splitting laugh can relieve tension in the body for nearly an hour afterwards.
- **Laughter boosts the immune system.** It decreases stress hormones and increases immune cells and infection-fighting antibodies, which helps to prevent disease.
- **Laughter releases those special endorphins, our 'feel-good' chemicals.** These promote general wellbeing and have even been known to reduce pain for a short time.
- **Laughter increases blood flow.** Blood flow keeps your heart nice and healthy.
- **Laughter calms you down when you are feeling distressed or angry.** Using laughter in this way can diffuse a situation more quickly than most strategies. It also helps you to move on from the initial conflict.
- **Laughter has even been shown to help people live longer!**

Here are some simple yet engaging ideas you can use in the classroom to increase the laughter levels and boost positivity in your classes. Why not try out one or two to get you started and gauge the temperature of the room once you've done so?

- **The daily joke:** Share a joke with your classes every day. It may not be that funny, but that in itself will be funny to them. You'll be amazed at how quickly the mood in a room can change when you focus on some humour.
- **Smile upon arrival:** I cannot emphasise this enough. Smiling as your students enter will ensure they smile too. It's infectious, remember!
- **Amusing stories:** Share funny anecdotal stories with your class. Students love listening to stories – the funnier the better. Add a little warmth to their day.
- **Funny video clips:** Share funny video clips with your tutees during form time. There's nothing better than ending the day laughing together. YouTube has some wonderful examples to share if you do some digging and animal clips seem to be a firm favourite of young people.
- **Comical books:** Choose books to read with comical characters or events in them. There is nothing quite like the pure joy of an entire class laughing at a book they are reading together.
- **Amusing resources:** Add a little humour to your lesson slides. I asked my teaching team to create Bitmoji characters of themselves for a display a couple of years ago and one or two of them have become a little obsessed with their creations. They appear on all their slides and the students love them.
- **Know your students:** In time, you will learn your students' sense of humour and you can use that to promote their wellbeing.
- **Student comics:** Ask students to share their own funny jokes, anecdotes, and book, film or television programme recommendations, explaining why they find their choice so funny with the class. The more contributions that are made, the merrier they will be.
- **Be human:** If something isn't going to plan, it's okay to laugh it off. Students are on your side. They'll laugh with you and it's so good for building effective relationships.

So, what are you waiting for? Go and spread some laughter with your class. In the words of the great John Cleese, 'A wonderful thing about true laughter is that it just destroys any kind of system of dividing people.' We all need a little more of that in our lives.

#alaughaminute
#connect
#smilesallround

Idea 37: Nature nurture

Spending time in nature reduces stress levels and leaves you more productive as a result.

I've lived in London for five years now, but I am and always will be a country girl at heart. I grew up in a tiny village in the Vale of Belvoir that consisted of one main street – the local shop was essentially someone's back room. There was no bus route through so if you wanted to go anywhere, you walked, cycled or drove. The thing I miss the most about that village is the silence. The pure serenity of hearing nothing at all.

I doubt very much that I will ever get used to the constant noise that comes from living in the capital, even if I do love the excitement of the place. I find myself craving nature during my busiest times. It's at these times that I find a wander in the park is just what I need to nurture and clear my mind. The fact that I crave nature is enough to tell me how powerful it is for my productivity and wellbeing, but here are a few more reasons why you may need it too:

- **Nature improves your short-term memory.** Studies have shown that a walk in the park or through a field is better for short-term memory than a walk along a busy street. This is because your brain still has to think about a lot when you are walking in a built-up area. It makes sense to find somewhere altogether more peaceful.
- **Nature boosts your mental energy.** A walk in nature can energise your mind and prepare you for another stint of work.
- **Nature is a known stress reliever.** Studies have shown that people who take to nature to relax have less cortisol (a hormone related to stress) in their bodies than those who don't.
- **Nature improves your concentration.** Many studies have proven this fact. Some even go so far as to suggest that just looking at images of nature has a positive effect on your concentration. (That must be why I spend so much time looking at stunning mountains on Instagram then!)
- **Nature can improve your creativity.** Studies have shown this to be true. So, if you're at a dead end with your lesson planning, take a break in nature and come back to it.

Getting students into nature

So, with all this in mind, how can we ensure students get these wonderful benefits? I delivered an assembly last year to Year 8 on adventures. I asked all 150 students if they had ever been to Hampstead Heath. Only about 15 of them raised their hands. The heath is two miles from the school. I was amazed. If we as educators aren't emphasising the importance of being outdoors, it appears many students won't get the message. Here are some suggestions to share with your students.

- **Lunchtime walk:** Encourage students to take a walk around the school field at lunchtime instead of staying indoors. The fresh air will clear their mind and invigorate them before afternoon lessons.
- **Local park wander:** Ask them to find their local park over the weekend and suggest their parents take them there. It's amazing what a bit of family outdoor bonding can do.
- **Download the app AllTrails:** This app is brilliant! It contains hundreds of different trails across the UK and internationally. Wherever they are in the country, this app will show them a nearby trail and offer full instructions about how to get there and which route to take once they've arrived. It's perfect for older students who wish to go exploring.
- **Organise nature-driven trips:** Why not take students to the nearest national park as a rewards trip? You'd be surprised at how many have never been, but have a fantastic time when they are there.
- **Nature challenge:** Set students a half term homework that involves seeking out nature. It could include a checklist of things to find, like different types of tree or a kissing gate or stile, for example.
- **Geocaching fun:** Encourage students to go Geocaching. Geocaching is awesome. It is literally treasure hunting using directions from an app. Ask them to download the app and go hunting with their parents or guardians.
- **Tell the parents:** Speak to parents at parents' evening about the importance of the outdoors. Parents hold the key to more students experiencing nature and its stress-busting benefits.

Next steps

At the height of exam season, why not consider taking students to the local park for a boost of nature and the chance to do some meditation breathing? See Idea 31 for more on this.

#naturenurture
#exercise
#powerofnature

Idea 38: Stress-free sanctuary

Creating a calm and stress-free space ensures students receive important downtime.

Rebeka Aylwin, sociology teacher and head of the humanities faculty at Oriel High School, shares her advice on creating a stress-free space.

It is likely that many students are not getting enough sleep (see Idea 39: Sleep easy for more specific ideas on how to solve this). Lack of sleep can have a negative impact on students' ability to concentrate and recall information. Reducing stress and increasing sleep will have a significant effect on their overall wellbeing, as well as their ability to revise. One way that students can help to control their stress levels is by controlling their environment, which can make their working time more productive and their recharge time more restful. What follows are ideas for students to help create a positive working environment and a stress-free sanctuary.

Let there be light!

Especially in the morning. Exposing ourselves to light first thing tells our bodies that it's time to start the day. Get students to open their curtains as soon as they wake up to absorb some energising natural light, which can be an instant mood (and immunity) booster. The opposite is true later in the day and we should try to have as little light exposure as possible in the evening. Darkening your evenings tells your body that it's going to be time for sleep soon. Encouraging students to use a side lamp, or even investing in a red-light bulb, will find them being much drowsier before bedtime.

Minimise clutter

Having a good tidy up can be a therapeutic activity in itself, and can help students to be able to find what they need more quickly, boost productivity and creativity, and give them more space to work in. There are a range of ways you can help students to achieve this – try setting them one of the following challenges:

1. Set a timer for five minutes and see how much you can tidy away.
2. Go through your wardrobe and see if there's anything you could donate to charity.

3. Create a decluttering checklist to do over the next week. Suggest they take before and after pictures to share with their friends to celebrate their accomplishments.

Tidy away work

Ideally, we should be encouraging students, where they can, to revise outside of the bedroom and keep that as a separate space for sleep and relaxation. However, for a lot of students, revising in their bedroom is unavoidable, and if space is limited they may have to sit on their beds to work. Tell students to make sure that all work and revision materials are tidied away and put out of sight before they start getting ready for bed. This helps to create a symbolic barrier that tells them that work is done, and sleep is on its way.

Bring the outdoors in

Natural elements such as plants, flowers, wood, rocks and stones can help to promote creativity and relaxation. This can be said for your own classroom as well as students' homes and bedrooms. Look for plants that filter indoor pollutants, such as areca, bamboo, lady palms, rubber plants, peace lilies and spider plants. Plants are shown to reduce stress as well as creating a feeling of overall wellbeing.

Calming colour schemes

Whilst redecorating their bedrooms is an unlikely option for most students, looking at the colour schemes of their accessories and furnishings is more practicable. Colour can be used as a stress management tool and shades of green and blue are shown to reduce levels of anxiety and calm the mind. Using these colours for items such as cushions, rugs, lamps or a warm fleece blanket to snuggle under when relaxing can increase feelings of harmony for students. Encourage students to create their own abstract artwork on a blank canvas using these colours.

Soothing scents

Our sense of smell is closely linked to our memory and using smell to create a tranquil environment is common practice for relaxation and meditation. Older students may be responsible enough to use candles with their parents' permission, but a safer alternative is an essential oil diffuser or room spray. Use rosemary to help improve concentration and focus, lavender for relaxation, geranium to uplift mood and balance emotions, and eucalyptus to refresh the mind.

Making simple changes by following all or some of these tips can help towards creating a peaceful environment for many students. This step towards reducing stress can have so many positive knock-on effects, including improving sleep, enhancing energy levels and motivation, lifting mood levels and increasing immunity.

Next steps

This is a big project to take on board all at once, so why not start with one or two of the ideas? Encourage students to pick a zone in their room that they will work towards making calm and peaceful and ask them to report back to you once it's done.

#stressfreezone
#declutter
#peaceful

Idea 39: Sleep easy

Supporting students to have enough sleep is paramount to their success in school.

We've all been there. The drilling sound of your alarm goes off and you can barely open your eyes. Heavy with exhaustion, you drag yourself to work to take part in a five-period day with a duty on top. It's safe to say you're going to find the day more difficult than usual. Now imagine what it must be like for our students who, for whatever reason, have also had very little sleep and need to take on board new content, challenging questions and high expectations from teachers. It is just as important for our students to get enough sleep as it is for us. Here's why.

- Sleep improves students' mental, emotional and physical performance.
- Sleep improves the immune system, balances hormones, boosts the metabolism and improves brain function.
- Allowing seven to eight hours of sleep a night clears the brain, ready for a new day of learning.

Here are some sleeping tips for students:

- **Switch it off:** Encourage students to switch off any electrical devices by at least 9pm every night. Many young people play computer games late into the night – we should be warning them of the dangers of this.
- **Phone sense:** Encourage students to charge their phone outside of the bedroom. That way they won't be tempted to scroll mindlessly through Snapchat or TikTok late into the evening.
- **Cut out the snacks:** Ensure students are aware of the impact sugary snacks can have upon sleep. The less of these they have in the evening, the better their sleep will be.
- **Essential oils:** Explain the value of essential oils like lavender. A sprinkle of this on a pillow can improve sleep patterns.
- **Reading:** This is such an effective way to calm students down before they drift off.

#sleepeasy
#sweetdreams

> **Next steps**
> Take a survey to find out the sleep patterns of your tutees. From there, you can make a plan of action to support their sleep!

Chapter 4

Learning
legends

Tried and tested learning methods help students progress quickly and confidently through their education. This chapter is full of them!

As educators, of course we want the best possible learning experience for our students. That means knowing which learning methods work best and when to use them. Having taught for over ten years now, I can tell you I've had my fair share of learning disasters in my classroom. Who hasn't? From ridiculous pseudoscience theories like brain gym to the crazy notion of triple marking, neither of which had any impact on the learning of the students I taught. Thankfully, those are relics of the yesteryear of education. Today I, along with many other educators, have come to know the power of effective learning methods.

This chapter contains ideas that support the best possible learning outcomes for students, such as the concept of live modelling, the power of knowledge organisers and the impressive effects of low-stakes quizzing. It also focuses on the learning environment and how to make the most of the learning spaces you are given. Take a look and see what would work in your own classroom.

Idea 40: Classroom care

Creating a calm learning space promotes students' wellbeing and builds their confidence to learn.

A classroom should be an inspiring space. It should be interactive and useful to promote learning, as well as being a calm environment that supports student wellbeing. It's often best to keep the wall at the front of the classroom free from too many fussy displays, in order to keep students focused on the task at hand when needed, but having classroom displays elsewhere aids learning, increases enjoyment and encourages students to take pride in their work.

One important aim when teaching is to create independent learners. Part of that involves providing learning aids around the room and directing students to make good use of them.

Students should feel familiar enough with your room to know where they can get help and resources from without disturbing the class.

Here are some ideas to help you prepare your classroom so that it is a space that inspires and supports student learning and wellbeing.

Key words and vocabulary banks

These will be most useful in subjects where students need to remember complex vocabulary and definitions. If we want students to use the terminology of our subject areas, we need to expose them to it. Display space is an effective way to do this.

Sentence support

Try including useful sentence starters on your displays to encourage less able students to become confident when writing. They can use them to formulate verbal responses and extended writing pieces.

Reflection

You could dedicate some display space to show the different ways in which students can mark their work using green pens for reflection.

Seeing the modelled examples around them can trigger their understanding of the importance of feedback and reflection. Using a different-coloured pen for reflection and improvement is a common strategy in many secondary schools. This will enable them to see and understand the value of reflection.

Posters

I love these, and so do the students. My posters are based around the subject I teach (English), but you can tailor them to your own subject or school phase. They breathe imagination into the room, and serve as useful reminders of past learning.

Student work

There's always room for this, and you could occupy corridor space too, as student work will then get a much wider audience. Instead of throwing away old revision creations, you could frame them, along with a photo of the students who made them. This gives students a sense of achievement and pride, whilst encouraging others to work hard too.

Resource station

Have a station in your room where students have access to any resources they may need, for example glue, rulers, paper, mark schemes and homework challenges. That way, they don't need to disturb anyone by asking for help during tasks; they can simply help themselves.

Wall of Humanity

Another option is to create a 'Wall of Humanity'. This is a working wall containing students' thoughts and feelings about particular events that take place throughout the year, such as Remembrance Sunday. Students have the opportunity to share their opinions and reflect, and you can add to this whenever you are discussing recent events.

Seating arrangements

An effective seating plan can have a hugely beneficial influence on your students. There are two things to consider when thinking about where your students sit. Firstly, the table arrangements. I tend to teach my students in rows, but occasionally, I will switch to a horseshoe design. Personally, I find having all students facing me an effective way to teach as it encourages all students to face the front and concentrate. Next, you must consider your seating plan. As a rule, allowing students to sit next to their friends is not always a positive learning experience for them. The temptation to talk may lead to distractions and less learning opportunity. It is often easier to set a seating plan designed to get the most out of the students, so that the learning which takes place is successful. A well-thought-through seating plan can make all the difference to a lesson.

Comfy corner

You could also use spaces as a positive behaviour management tool. Something your students will love is a 'comfy corner'. This can consist of two comfy chairs (taken stealthily from the staffroom) and two bookcases filled with books. Students can then take it in turns to sit there and read during reading lessons. You can use it as a reward for exemplary effort too and it will become a place that students will work hard to get to.

Next steps
Consider the layout of your classroom. What resources are available for your students? Can students see their work on display? Are the seating arrangements supporting you to get the most out of your students? If not, consider a rethink about your classroom design.

#classroomcare
#connect

Idea 41: The writing is on the door

Small, simple gestures show you care.

One of the best purchases I ever made was a self-adhesive whiteboard. I wanted one to stick on my classroom door, initially with the idea that I could use it to leave messages for any snails who were late to the lesson only to find we had eloped to the computer room. However, over the years it has become far more useful in a number of ways.

I use it to pose open-ended questions for students to ponder as they line up. It works perfectly as it gives students something to do while they wait silently to enter, and allows students time to seriously consider the question at a deeper level. In short, it promotes higher-order thinking skills. By the time they are settled in the classroom, all the students have had time to think and are ready for a full-blown discussion, often about challenging issues or divergent thinking. It also provides the perfect lead-in to your lesson. Not only that, it makes for a very quick start too.

I also use it to write positive messages to students as they arrive. They might have done particularly well in a recent assessment, or they may have exams coming up. The board message cheers them up during times that could be stressful for them. It's lovely to see their smiles as they read it. Students feel a real sense of pride if they receive a special mention.

The board is used for literacy riddles too. I write the riddle on the board in the morning and students from across the school find me during the day to tell me they have figured it out. My younger students absolutely love this. They rush to class to be first to see the riddle. Often, I will hand out house points for those who are first to solve it.

You should all have one of these outside your classroom. You can find them easily in hardware stores or pound shops. They promote learning, encourage participation and make students feel good. Just watch out for colleagues who think it's funny to draw funky pictures (amongst other things!) of you on it.

#learn
#connect

Idea 42: Low-stakes retrieval testing

Low-stakes retrieval supports students' knowledge retention and creates success.

Low-stakes retrieval is essentially checking that students have understood subject content on a regular basis through questions designed to be answered in a short, concise way. It has been known for some years now that low-stakes retrieval is beneficial for students' knowledge retention. Studies have shown time and again that there are many benefits to introducing regular retrieval practice into the classroom. One recent study carried out by Roediger, Putman and Smith (2011) found a plethora of benefits, such as better retention, enhanced identification of knowledge gaps, a stronger transfer of knowledge to new contexts, a willingness for students to learn more and a better organisation of knowledge.

With so many positive outcomes to low-stakes retrieval, any teacher would be remiss not to embed this activity into their daily teaching practice. Here are some ways in which you can do this.

1. **Mini retrieval quizzes as starters:** Begin each lesson by having students enter the classroom, sit in silence and take a quiz. Questions could include knowledge from the previous lesson, week or unit. The more connections students make, the higher the chance of them remembering the information in the future.
2. **Summarising:** At the beginning or end of a lesson, week or topic, ask students to summarise their learning. This works well if you give specific instructions. For example, 'summarise Act One of Romeo and Juliet in 50 words'. This requires students to focus on only the key information in order to be concise. Show them your own summary once they have completed the task so they can check and amend their own work.
3. **Pre-unit tests:** Ask students to answer a series of questions about the topic or unit you are about to begin teaching. Studies have shown that this activity actually helps with retention later on as students have been primed. It is also a great way for the teacher to gauge the stage of learning each student is at and plan follow-up lessons accordingly.
4. **Self-quizzing:** Ask students to write their own questions in the margin of their work in order to test themselves later. This not only

supports retention but encourages independent learning as well. Students can come back to these any time they like and they are very handy when it comes to revision season.

5. **Paper quiz:** Hand students a quiz and ask them to complete it in a certain amount of time. This allows you to circulate the room and spot any common misconceptions or correct errors as you go.

6. **Paired quiz:** Have students create a list of questions and then quiz each other. Give them a time frame and have them move around the room quizzing each other as they go. This ensures all students are testing at the same time.

7. **Interrogation quizzing:** This involves students being asked to elaborate on their answers by responding to 'why?' or 'how?' questions. This can be done at the end of a starter quiz where you want the students to demonstrate a greater depth of understanding. It could also be used during paired quizzing.

8. **Modelling:** Ask students to demonstrate how they would answer an exam question by talking the class through it step-by-step. Instruct them to talk about what they are doing and why as they complete the activity. Students in the class listening should be following the demonstration and taking their own notes as they go. This is a great way for students to perfect exam technique. It also works really well for practical subjects.

9. **Mind maps:** Ask students to make a mind map of a topic you have recently studied within a certain timeframe. They must be instructed to make links as they go. Once completed, students check and amend their work by referring to reliable sources of sound information.

10. **Image recall:** As a starter or plenary, place a number of images related to a topic on the board and ask students to silently write an explanation for the images. Once completed, share your own example for reference. This is a great way to trigger students' memory and recall information.

11. **Graphs and charts:** These are perfect for synthesising information that students must recall from memory. The more they reorganise the information, the more likely they are to remember it.

12. **Timelines:** Getting your students to create timelines is another quick and accurate way to recall information and measure their memory.

Next steps
Why not start a low-stakes daily quiz in your lessons to encourage and aid retention?

#lowstakesretrievalquizzing
#learn

Idea 43: Knowledge organisers

Knowledge organisers support the learning and retention of key information.

Knowledge organisers have gained popularity over the last few years and it's no wonder with the great benefits they afford students, not only when it comes to learning, but also revising. Joe Kirby was the first person to blog about them (to my knowledge) and to put it simply he stated, a knowledge organiser (KO) sets out the important, useful and powerful knowledge on a topic on a single page. They are most effective when all of the information is on one side of A4, but two sides of A4 would also suffice.

So, what are the benefits?

- Teachers can decide which content is important and which to leave out, making learning specific and meaningful.
- Students can refer to the content throughout the teaching of the topic or unit.
- Content is collated and organised in a clear, memorable way.
- Students are left feeling confident about the topic or unit they are studying.

Here's what to consider when creating a knowledge organiser.

Purpose

Why are you creating the knowledge organiser? What purpose does it serve? In most cases this will be to create a foundation of knowledge for students to learn from and be able to retrieve at a later date. Knowledge organisers are a great tool to use in order to transfer content from the short-term memory into the long-term memory. Careful construction of the knowledge organiser allows students to learn content effectively.

Content

The next step to consider is what content to include on the knowledge organiser. This is no easy task as you need to weigh up the fact that the knowledge must fit comfortably onto one side of A4 paper against the masses of content to choose from for each topic. Powerful knowledge, as defined by Michael Young (2013) in 'On the powers of powerful knowledge', is specialised knowledge rather than general, and is differentiated from the experiences of students. Therefore, the choice about what to include needs careful consideration. This should take into consideration the needs of the end goal: how the students will be assessed at the end of the unit. Is there any point including contextual information on the organiser, which would no doubt be useful for a 19th-century novel for example, if you aren't going to assess the students' knowledge of this at the end of the unit?

Presentation

Another consideration would be the presentation of the information. Many organisers list information and have separate sections for each subsection of information. This can be useful for retrieval practice, but also consider the need for the information to link together in some way. The design of the page should suit the needs of the way in which the information will be referred to throughout the teaching of the unit.

Pedagogy

The final area to consider is the pedagogy of knowledge organisers. They are only useful tools if they are referred to during teaching at regular intervals. There are a few ways in which this can be achieved.

Retrieval practice is a great way to ensure the knowledge of the organisers is returned to and recalled frequently. Low-stakes quizzing of the knowledge, timelines of events, fill the missing gaps, charts and graphs are all ways in which the content can be revisited (see Idea 42: Low-stakes retrieval testing for more on this). This kind of testing will also help you to identify any gaps in student knowledge, which can be revisited in future lessons.

In order for students to fully understand the knowledge contained on the organisers, it is important to create a deeper level of knowledge about each piece of information listed. This elaboration of content is then likely to be recalled when the knowledge organiser triggers this information. Depth of discussion during teaching supports this aim. During this teaching, it is important to connect ideas and information together. This type of retrieval practice is often called elaborative interrogation and there must be active understanding and meaningful consideration of what is being learnt (see Daniel Willingham's 2014 book *Why Don't Students Like School?*).

To ensure knowledge organisers really serve their purpose, ask students to reorganise the information in some way. The more the students synthesise the knowledge, the more likely they are to remember it and store it in their long-term memory. By reordering the information using activities like ranking, connecting themes and ideas, and presenting it differently, students are transferring it to their long-term memory and therefore stand a better chance of remembering the information.

By undertaking all of the above regularly, students have a high chance of retaining the information. This is made even more likely by the use of explicit instruction. Model everything you ask them to do at every opportunity. Kat Howard advocates a 'me, we, you, we, you' approach to this. By allowing students to understand the process of retrieval and use of knowledge organisers, they are much more likely to be successful at this on their own.

Next steps

Why not deliver training to a team of teachers to ensure everyone understands the purpose and role of knowledge organisers? Work together with your team to produce one for each unit. This will save you hours of time and spreads the workload whilst also developing each teacher.

#learn #knowledgeispower

Idea 44: Whole-class feedback

Using whole-class feedback effectively ensures students make quicker progress in their work, which gives them motivation and confidence.

Done well, whole-class feedback provides accurate, timely, useful and actionable feedback to students. Here's how it works.

1. When marking a set of books, instead of writing the same comment over and over again, note down common misconceptions that students make as well as any commonly misspelt words. This information should be shared with the class using a whole-class feedback slide or resource at the start of the next lesson.
2. Consider how these misconceptions can be addressed in the next lesson by asking students to complete a learning activity. For example, if students have written an essay and are having a particular problem with use of complex sentences, explain the common misconception that they had and then teach them how to use complex sentences effectively using a series of learning activities.
3. At this point, students will be able to go back to their original work and correct their errors, but they will also be able to use the newly taught knowledge in future work too.
4. A word of caution. As Daisy Christodoulou explains in her blog 'Whole-class feedback: improve the curriculum, not just the pupil', doing this can lead to the discovery of further misconceptions. Make a note of these further misconceptions for future curriculum development. The feedback here is for the teacher, not the student. When marking, decide which misconceptions can be taught easily and are for the students and which need planning into the curriculum and so are for the teacher.

For me, whole-class feedback has been a game changer. Not only have I saved literally hours of time (and ink!), but student progress has also sped up and the accuracy of their writing has dramatically improved. This, in turn, boosts their motivation and confidence in their own work.

Next steps

Read Dylan Wiliam's *Embedded Formative Assessment* to learn more about whole-class feedback.

#wholeclassfeedback
#learn

Idea 45: Intervention engagement

For intervention to be effective, you must achieve buy-in.

Intervention strategies usually take place when gaps in student learning have been identified, often in the run-up to exam season. Interventions can take place during normal school lessons or in extra after-school sessions. When planned and delivered effectively, they can have a significant impact on the attainment and progress of students. There are many approaches to interventions, but one thing is clear: intervention simply won't work if the students involved are not invested. Intervention ensures students feel confident and ready for exams, as it allows them to close any knowledge gaps and solidify their learning.

In this idea, Liam Davis, a teacher at Woodside High, Wood Green, London explains how they managed to get students on board by making intervention at their school fun.

Getting student buy-in

Buy-in is key to ensuring students not making expected progress are receiving support. Intervention is often seen as 'extra' by students, which can put them off engaging with it initially.

Firstly, it is important to identify the correct students for intervention. At our school, we created a group called Key 30. This was a focus group of students who were about to embark upon Year 11 with lower attainment and/or progress than expected. The Key 30 became an individual tutor group. They were given an extra one-hour lesson in English, maths and science respectively. They were also given lessons on wellbeing and careers education. These lessons took place in the morning and they continued to receive booster classes in the afternoon for their other subjects. This meant their school day began at 7.40am and finished at 4.30pm. A tall order for 30 underperforming 15- and 16-year-olds, but that's where the next step comes into play.

Once you have your group and timetable set up, the next step is to gain buy-in from the students. At Woodside High, we did this in several ways.

- **Residential trips across the year:** We created three of these, one for maths, one for English and one for science. Each was themed. Subject teachers attended weekend residentials that involved lessons, of course, but also activities such as rock climbing, skiing and potholing. The time spent outside even influenced the learning activities that took place, particularly in English where students improved their descriptive writing skills. These trips showed the students how much we believed in them and wanted them to succeed, as well as cementing strong relationships between staff and students.
- **Food and drink:** We wanted to offer students much-needed sustenance whilst they studied. For example, refreshments and food were made available for those students attending the early morning lessons. The Key 30 group became so popular that headteacher, Gerry Robinson, and myself were both asked by other students if they could join and often this was allowed.
- **Rewards:** Trips to Nando's at the end of each term worked well, as well as rewards for students who had 100 per cent attendance and punctuality or who had shown hard work and commitment.
- **Creating a team ethic:** Staff and students alike felt as though they were in it together.
- **Innovation:** Last, but certainly not least, creating challenging, innovative lessons in order to avoid students hitting the snooze button at 6.30am was vital. Gathering leading speakers such as Martin Tyler from Sky Sports and having science teachers conduct experiments before daylight and English teachers taking students to Alexandra Palace to describe the world around them all helped to get students out of bed in the morning.

The result of all the hard work by both staff and students was that the 2018 cohort of Key 30 students all left with a healthy grade across English, maths and science. By making it fun and engaging, students got the results to enable them to move on to the next stage of their lives.

Next steps

Consider targeting students across the entire school with some of these ideas. Early intervention ensures that young people are given the support they need sooner rather than later. Identify their needs, deliver an effective intervention programme and have some fun along the way!

#funintervention
#learn
#volunteer

Idea 46: Homework

Homework should be valued, relevant, organised and consistent in order to receive buy-in from students and reduce stress levels for both teachers and students.

Homework can be a source of stress for both teachers and students alike. If homework is to be something in which all students participate, it must be valued, relevant, organised and consistent.

Homework must be valued

What is the point of homework?

- It teaches students to work independently and become more self-disciplined.
- It teaches students to take responsibility and develop initiative.
- It teaches students how to manage their time effectively.
- It teaches students to review and practise what has been covered in class.
- It teaches students how to use resources such as: libraries, the internet, and reference materials.
- It allows parents and guardians to take an active role in their child's progress and learning.
- It allows parents and guardians to see what their child is learning and promotes healthy communication and relationships at home.

Homework must be relevant

Students will not value homework if they cannot make the connection between what they are learning in lessons and what you ask them to do at home. So, it makes sense that whatever task you set ties in with the class learning. Examples of relevant homework include:

- Homework that reviews the learning which has taken place. This can be done in many ways: summary tasks, extended writing, mind maps, and so on.

- Revision of the key words or vocabulary you have taught students that week. Include a retrieval task which tests their knowledge of this in the next lesson.
- Contextual resources that need to be read before you start a topic. Quiz students on the resource as a retrieval task before you begin a new topic.
- Spelling lists to revise from. Again, use retrieval to ensure students have revised the words.

Homework must be organised and consistent

This can be difficult when there are many subjects across the school setting homework, but it need not be. Ensure you have a specific day on which you always set your homework task, and never deviate from this. If students know which day homework is set, they are much more likely to remember to do it as they are in a regular routine. It is far less stressful for students when they know what to expect. Like many initiatives in schools, consistency is key.

#homework
#learn

Idea 47: Live modelling

Davina Canham, an English teacher and lead practitioner at Kettering Buccleuch Academy, explains how live modelling can create confident and happy writers.

What is it?

Live modelling is a powerful process in which teachers model the high standards that they expect their students to achieve during a live writing activity in the lesson.

Why do it?

We expect students to put pen to paper every single day. For those reluctant writers in our classes this can be a daunting process. Live modelling allows you to share and demonstrate the process of thinking to produce a model response that all students feel capable of accessing. In sharing standards, students can see what they are aiming for and the processes and thinking needed to get there. Sharing models or student work can help with student confidence and help them to gauge where they are currently at and what they need to do next to achieve the level of that modelled example. Furthermore, introducing new vocabulary can be done gradually to raise the quality of writing, through applying new vocabulary such as discourse markers or other subject-specific terminology. By talking through and weighing up ideas and choices, students are able to come along on the journey to the finished piece, whether that be an introduction, analysis or other text type. As highlighted by Professor Barak Rosenshine, this practice has a marked impact on student progress.

How is it done?

Before embarking on the live model, discuss with your class what you aim to cover in the response and what knowledge or skills you want to demonstrate. Then, take each stage of the modelling process step-by-step, ensuring students are following and listening to the instructions correctly.

Why might teachers feel worried about this process?

As the expert in the room, you may feel under pressure when writing models live in front of a class. Other valid concerns could be that behaviour may slip during this process or that you will not get any useful feedback from your class. Finally, you may be worried that they themselves might make mistakes or are not experienced enough to produce models of the highest calibre. Start by looking at the steps below to alleviate these.

Ways to alleviate concerns

The easiest option starting as a 'rookie modeller' is to use a writing model from an exam board exemplar, of which there are many available on exam board websites, and talk students through it. Moving on from this you could have an exam board model where there are gaps which students discuss and the class decide what to put in. To avoid getting limited input from students, you can ask a question about the next section and allow for discussion and note taking by students to clarify their thoughts. Furthermore, engendering a culture of making mistakes and editing is thoroughly encouraged: deliberately make mistakes for the students to spot and correct for you! When crafting the response your thought processes and decision making can be stated out loud. As you model, consider saying things like:

- What should I write next?
- How can we develop this?
- Is there evidence for this that I can add in?
- What impact does this have?
- Should we put in a discourse marker here?
- How could this be changed to be more precise?
- What is a better word to use rather than 'this'?
- Does this make sense? Can we change it?
- Have we covered context?
- What alternative could we now include?
- Do I need punctuation here?

Modelling varieties

There is a variety of methods or approaches you can follow with live modelling. For example, having a single list of vocabulary or sentence prompts displayed by the side of the live model, as a sort of *aide-memoire*, is helpful. This structures or aids your own thought process whilst demonstrating the use of analytical or evaluative vocabulary. This can be linked to the question or criteria and can be referenced as a challenge for students to use the phrases or vocabulary, when in fact it is there to prompt the teacher. Either way it's a win. Another strategy is to pre-pick the quotation or evidence and type out some sentence starters which could be added to by the class in the lesson. This could then be colour-coded or annotated to show how it features the assessment objectives. The I-We-You model in practice is a powerful thing. Once students have seen and picked apart a model with teacher guidance (I), contributed to the class model with scaffolding and discussion (We), they can then attempt their own or in pairs (You) with perhaps some prompts or key words on the board.

Next steps

This process can eventually become a checklist once students are comfortable with writing their own introductions. As a result, they will create more conceptual and featured thesis statements, which, in turn, will bolster their confidence levels and well-being. Students will become confident enough to use the process you have been through as a class, create their own questions and model with their peers. These models can be captured as a revision resource for later on in the year or put on display. As more and more students became assured in knowing the standard you are aiming for and how to get there, the better the responses will be due to your shared journey.

#livemodelling
#learn

Idea 48: Direct vocabulary instruction

Students with a rich vocabulary and the knowledge of how to use it feel confident and happier with their work.

Over the years, I have developed my own practice to include two powerful approaches with regards to teaching students about vocabulary. I have seen their work improve significantly and their confidence to communicate using a rich, wide volume of ambitious words go from strength to strength. The two approaches go hand-in-hand with each other and are, namely, exposing students to Tier 2 vocabulary and direct vocabulary instruction. The importance of teaching students effective ways to communicate through developing a rich vocabulary should not be underestimated. In her book, *Bringing Words to Life*, Professor Isabel Beck argues that there is a vast difference between vocabulary knowledge among learners of different ability or socioeconomic groups. She believes that, unless teachers intervene with vocabulary instruction, this difference remains with students as they grow and become adults.

What is Tier 2 vocabulary?

Beck introduces a three-tiered model to support understanding of vocabulary instruction:

- **Tier 1:** Most basic words which typically appear in oral conversations, such as warm, cat, girl, swim. Learners are exposed to these words from a very young age, so readily become familiar with them and are likely to use them in their everyday language.
- **Tier 2:** Words which are of high utility for mature language users and are found across a variety of domains, such as precede, auspicious, retrospect. As these words are characteristic of written text, and used more rarely in conversation, students are less likely to learn these words independently. This is why Tier 2 words are thought of as being the most productive approach, with the aim of teaching around 400 new words per year.
- **Tier 3:** Rarely used words which are limited to specific topics and domains, such as photosynthesis, machicolations. These words are

probably best learned when a specific need arises, such as teaching subject-specific terminology in the context of a lesson.

Once clear on the different tiers of vocabulary, it is time to decide which Tier 2 words to use and why. Firstly, how important is the word chosen? Does it have a strong utility? Can it be conceptually understood and will it be well suited to instructional teaching? The simple questions below can help you when deciding which words to choose.

1. How useful is it? Will students meet it often? Will they find it in other texts? Will they use it to describe their own experiences?
2. How does it relate to other words they know? Will it add more depth to a topic?
3. What does the word contribute in the situation or text?

What is direct vocabulary instruction?

In the past, I have often taught students new words by sharing the word and its definition; showing them an example sentence containing the new word; executing match-up activities; and then asking them to use it in their own writing. Since reading about direct and robust vocabulary instruction, I have learnt that this does not go far enough in order for the new vocabulary to be adopted successfully. Beck argues that robust vocabulary instruction, which 'involves directly explaining the meanings of words along with thought-provoking, playful and interactive follow-up', is a more effective way of teaching students to adopt new vocabulary. It is important that the new words are seen multiple times in a frequent manner using various different ways. This ensures that the learning activities involve deep processing from the students.

Here are some ideas to try.

- Students have log books to record any new words and their meanings. They could also write down examples of the word being used.
- Share with students one correct example and one incorrect example of the word to establish meaning. Question the students on the correct use and be sure to dig for an explanation.
- Pair recently learnt words which don't directly relate to each other. Ask students if a relationship exists. This supports students' understanding of the word in a new and unfamiliar context. For example, *Juliet is seen as* **audacious** *when she goes against her*

parents' wishes, **subverting** *the traditional role of women during the Elizabethan era.*

- Share slightly altered definitions of words with students over the first few lessons of learning them. This prevents them from rote learning one definition and encourages them to think more deeply about the multiple contexts in which the word could be used. For example, **ambitious**.
  1. *Really wanting to succeed in becoming rich or important.*
  2. *Wanting to get ahead by becoming powerful.*
  3. *Wanting great success in life.*
- Try 'beat the clock' games. Give students two minutes to state either true or false to words used in different contexts or using a range of definitions. This deepens their understanding of the words. For example, *Benvolio is a* **sagacious** *character.* **Aloof** *people enjoy spending time with others.* **Generosity** *is a trait of* **avaricious** *people.*
- Use sentence stems containing newly learnt words. For example, *The* **enmity** *between the two characters...*

Both Tier 2 vocabulary exposure and specific instruction are now firmly embedded across every department in my school; as a result, students are empowered and their progress has gone from strength to strength.

> ### Next steps
> Why not start one lesson a week with a vocabulary challenge to get your students comfortable with using Tier 2 vocabulary on a regular basis?

#tiertwo
#wordmagic
#learn

Idea 49: Visualiser top tips

Visualisers ensure that students learn effectively and efficiently when used well.

I have already mentioned the use of visualisers in Idea 23: Visualiser vision on page 32 with regard to recognising student work, but here Fe Brewer, English teacher at Rawlins Academy in Loughborough, shares her top tips for brilliant student learners.

Once you've treated yourself to a visualiser, it's time to get playing. Like anything else, the more you use it, the more you'll realise you can do with it. Before you know it, you'll have forgotten how you taught without one! Here are some of the most effective ways I've used mine to support my students.

Have your own exercise book for each class you teach

I can't take credit for this idea – that deservedly goes to Kat Howard and a tweet she posted in late 2019. One of the most useful things you can do is keep a book for each of your classes.

There are many benefits to doing this: it's great for keeping track of what you've covered; it's useful for absentees who need to 'catch up'; and it's a good record of your teaching practice.

Perhaps most usefully, it serves as a resource bank, particularly when you want to return to knowledge or skills you've already covered and weave previous learning into your current lesson, sharing it with students on the visualiser. Rather than providing new resources, you can refer to those which students are already familiar with. Without getting into the science, this not only 'piggy-backs' on existing knowledge, but it also helps students to really consolidate their knowledge and realise the relationships between different pieces of work, exam questions or curriculum content. I have model paragraphs and plans that I return to time and time again, saving time and capitalising on pre-existing knowledge. Use your visualiser to share these models and return to them when students demonstrate misconceptions.

Worksheets galore: folding and gluing

Have you ever heard one of these phrases: 'Can you fold this for me?', 'Ah, I've got glue everywhere!', 'I can't cut straight'? I have. Too many times.

The truth is, there are students who don't possess skills and knowledge when it comes to – what we would consider to be – simple tasks. We could roll our eyes, scoff and belittle students for this because, to us, it seems trivial. Of course, it isn't trivial to the 15-year-old in front of us who has been doing their best to hide such a lack of skill for the last seven or eight years.

Demonstrating folding, cutting and sticking using a visualiser is easy, efficient and kind; it makes not knowing things seem less threatening when clearly demonstrated to everyone. We need to show students that they and their abilities matter, and that we have time to address their needs, no matter how simple. Little things like this can make a big difference when a young person feels inadequate, and can make all the difference when it comes to how much they value themselves and their place in the classroom.

Model, model, model

Another area I suspect we neglect is physical handling and navigating exam papers. I've lost count of how many students 'couldn't find' or 'missed' crucial questions in exams. Here again, your visualiser is your friend. Get a stack of full exam papers and slowly, explicitly, demonstrate how to navigate one: using the contents page, demonstrating page turning, tracking the words with your finger, underlining key words, planning and so on. We often assume students know how to do things and find information when they don't. Visualisers are key when it comes to modelling good practice because students can clearly see exactly how you – expert in the room – do things. This is great for the complex stuff, but we need to remember to model the simple but high-stakes stuff too.

Step-by-step

This one requires two bits of tech – your visualiser (or you could even do this one on Word or PowerPoint) and a projector remote with a 'freeze' function. The process is simple: provide your students sentence stems and support, one at a time, and construct paragraphs simultaneously as a class.

For example, you might offer students: 'Dickens portrays the character of Scrooge as…'. You then freeze your board. In a different colour, you and all of your students complete the sentence. Next, you take several answers from the class as well as sharing yours. You then move on to the next sentence structure, perhaps 'Dickens creates this impression through/by…', and freeze, write and share again. Repeat the process until everyone has an individual paragraph focused on a specific feature or interpretation that they are comfortable with. No one's answer is correct or incorrect (within reason), but they are all different. Along the way, students have shared answers and ideas, feeding back to one another and receiving live feedback from you too. Moreover, students will have seen the breadth of acceptable answers that a single question can hold – a valuable bonus when you have students who feel they shouldn't commit anything but 'the best answer' to paper.

So, what are you waiting for? Go get that visualiser and play!

#visualiserplay
#showme
#everydaymodelling
#simplematters
#doasido

Idea 50: Making a diagnosis

Diagnosing your students' performance throughout each unit of work will ensure they confidently know where they are at and how to progress.

Laura May Rowlands, head of faculty for English and Literacy at Woodlands Community College in Southampton, shares how she does this with her students.

Now that almost all subjects at GCSE are assessed by final exam, there is a need to ensure students understand where they are in terms of progression. This can no longer be ascertained through coursework or controlled assessment grades – and in any case we wouldn't expect students to have produced work at the start of a GCSE course that is the standard we would expect in that final exam. So how can we ensure that students understand the progress they are making and confidently remain focused on their long-term goal?

Diagnostic tasks

We all know the difference between formative and summative assessment, yet too often the methods we employ for these are the same. Creating a diagnostic task for each unit of learning helps to avoid this in several ways: it develops students' confidence in the tasks they are completing; allows for speedy and informative feedback; and, crucially, allows teachers to anticipate and precisely plan for existing gaps and emerging needs by prioritising a small section of knowledge or skill within a mark scheme, rather than focusing on the entire mark scheme itself. Think of it like this: if you are trying to give feedback on many things, you are at risk of simply 'verifying performance' (see Issue 8 of the *EGS Education Literature Bulletin* where David Didau and Nick Rose discuss 'What every teacher needs to know about psychology'), yet the key to success is often many seemingly insignificant factors being tied together. With a diagnostic task, you are aiming to remove an often-engrained focus on short-term performance and replace it with long-term proficiency.

So what is a diagnostic task?

In her book *Making Good Progress?*, Daisy Christodoulou argues that 'the drill and the performance are different and separate, but they are linked'. A diagnostic task necessarily, therefore, need not resemble an essay or practice exam question but should be carefully designed to take place after a judicious amount of input has taken place – say after two weeks of an eight-week unit – and should focus on a key piece of knowledge or skill. This then informs you as the teacher of key misconceptions or errors pertinent to your class. The task can take many forms: a multiple-choice quiz, a paragraph of writing, an annotated diagram, or an 'exploded quotation' (detailed analysis of a single quotation) – but, in order to quickly make a diagnosis and plan accordingly, it must be brief and completed in exam conditions. You could use the metaphor of a drill – after all, this is what professional sportspeople or musicians do to become proficient. Ensure students understand that they are practising a component of the final task, not the final task itself. All of the tasks listed above are sufficient to allow you, as the teacher, enough insight to see what you need to focus on next.

Feeding forward

When giving feedback, it is important to stress what it is you have been testing students' knowledge of. This can mean not giving a grade or number at all – you are not able to give an accurate mark or grade in any case, because you are not testing a 'whole' question. Some students may struggle with the idea of this – but make it clear that the number or grade isn't what needs to be focused on at this stage. Instead, the feedback needs to tightly focus on the gains which have been made between the start of the topic or unit and this diagnostic checkpoint – not how close to the final grade or target students are. Whole-class feedback can be of use here (see Idea 44: Whole-class feedback on page 71). Time then needs to be allocated for students to immediately act on this – whether this is through numbered feedback targets, a re-teach session, or picking apart a selection of responses as a class. Having seen all of your class's efforts, you will be able to identify specific weaknesses or patterns which you will have in mind throughout the rest of the unit too.

Building resilience

Getting students used to doing short tasks in exam conditions means the 'fear' of what they need to do lessens. It means they are confident when faced with a time-bound task and are used to receiving feedback on which they are obliged to act. Diagnostic tasks are also an excellent way to maintain a focus on their attitude to learning, through the effort you can see in the execution of each task. Presentation is an important factor too. Having the tasks set towards the start of the unit or topic means that students are able to self-regulate when preparing for their final assessment. What did they do well? What was their key misunderstanding or gap, and has that now been closed?

#diagnosistask
#whatwentwell
#knowledgesurgery

Idea 51: Wonderful writers

When students know how to write well, their confidence soars.

One of the biggest barriers to students' success in schools is their ability to articulate themselves clearly when they put pen to paper. Often, they have all the answers they need, but they struggle to formulate the right words and sentences when it comes to putting those ideas down on the page. The statistics regarding school leavers and literacy are staggering. Five million adults are functionally illiterate in the UK. One in four British five-year-olds struggle with basic vocabulary and three quarters of white working-class boys fail to reach the government's benchmark at the age of 16. Functionally illiterate adults are more likely to have self-esteem issues and social barriers. They may not be able to read books, letters, road signs, or even access the internet successfully. Illiteracy is also linked to shorter life expectancy, depression and obesity. These figures are depressing, but there is much we can do as educators to improve things. The responsibility of the literacy skills of young people lies with every teacher, not just those who teach English.

At my school, assistant headteacher Claire Thompson has been working hard to address this issue across the school. She has introduced an effective method of ensuring all teachers and students know how to construct a well-planned and formulated paragraph. We call this the T.M.C paragraph. The letters stand for Topic sentence, Main ideas, and Concluding sentence. Students in all subject areas are taught the power of a topic sentence, the importance of developing your topic sentence by including several pertinent ideas and the power of then summarising the view in the final concluding statement. This simple method has worked wonders with our students in all subject areas and teachers have commented on the improvements that students have made in their written assessments as a result of its introduction.

The method is introduced to students in the following format:

1. **Topic sentence:** A sentence that introduces the paragraph.
2. **Main ideas:** A series of sentences that all develop, explain and describe ideas linked to the topic sentence.
3. **Concluding sentence:** A powerful sentence that summarises the main ideas explored.

Here is a model of this in practice in a Year 9 English lesson:

Unit: Transactional writing
Topic: Gender inequality
Paragraph topic: Toxic masculinity

Topic sentence: Toxic masculinity is an example of the inequality that pressures men to suppress their emotions.
Main ideas: Have you ever seen a man holding tears back, pretending he's not hurt or simply laughing off any insults thrown his way? I know I have! When you expect a man to ignore any emotional pain, you are causing damage. Damage that is not only impactful on men but on women, too. It is logical that if society demands that men are brave, powerful and daring, women must be the opposite. This is not the case! It is not the case that men should not cry, nor that women should not be strong. It is not the case that men do not feel pain at the taunts they receive, nor that women are inferior. In 2019, suicide was the biggest killer of men aged 20 to 45 in the UK. Why? Because we expect men and boys to 'man-up' and suppress their emotions. This inequality is taking lives. When you shame someone into suppressing a natural emotion, you are risking condemning them to depression, despair and isolation.

Concluding sentence: Men deserve better!

The idea is simple and works efficiently and aptly in any lesson. The trick with getting this right with the students is to model, model, model. Without the teacher's expert guidance on this, students have a tendency to go off topic and perhaps might begin to consider ideas that are not relevant to or supportive of the main idea in their paragraph.

Next steps

Why not trial this with one of your classes? Follow the 'I-We-You' modelling process. This works in the following way. Firstly, live model on your own as the expert in the room. Next, model another idea together and finally, have students write their own idea using T.M.C. Before long, you will be sure to notice a measured difference in both the confidence and progress of your students' written skills.

#wonderfulwriters
#literacycounts
#learn

Idea 52: Planners at the ready

Encouraging students to use a planner leads to effective organisation and feelings of satisfaction at a day's schooling well done.

As teachers, we all use planners or diaries every day. I, for one, find it enormously difficult to remember meetings, training dates and after-school events, let alone which lessons I have each day, if I can't refer to my daily planner. In fact, I would go so far as to say that without it I feel genuine stress, related to not knowing what the day has in store and fear of forgetting something important. This is no different for the students we teach, so it is important they understand the need to plan ahead and stay organised. It is also vitally important that students learn to become less reliant on adults and more dependent on themselves as they mature throughout their education. Using a daily planner helps them to do this.

Embedding routines

Most students are issued with an academic year planner at the beginning of each year. If this is not the case, I urge you to encourage them to acquire one. For students to get the best out of their planner, they must be taught how to use it and it is vital routine use is established. Below are some ideas to get students used to this. I cannot emphasise enough the importance of embedding these early on in the year. Many students I come across haven't been taught the value of these useful books and so, throughout the year, they become of less and less importance and before they know it, the pages are blank for weeks on end. Here are some useful suggestions.

- **Morning registration:** Insist on planners being out on the table every form time. The first activity should be to review their day. This needs to be consistent for it to work.
- **Enquire:** Ask them about their day. What lessons do they have? Do they need to attend any after-school classes? Are they due to hand in homework? This encourages them to review their week too.
- **Afternoon registration:** Insist on planners being out every day. Ask students to review their day. There is usually a notes section on each week-view spread. Suggest they write down something they

learnt that inspired them or just a note about what they enjoyed most about the day. This encourages them to see the planner as a working document that they write in every day, even if home learning is not set.

- **Communication:** Communicate to parents in the planner. At my school, parents must sign the planner each week to show they are reviewing their child's work. I often write notes of thanks to parents or praise notes for things students have done well, which students love! It encourages them to take the planner home and show their parents.
- **Ban doodling!** Often students see these as their own personal doodling books. Encourage them to see them more as a professional organiser than a notebook. They will take more pride in it this way.
- **Quiz:** The planner usually contains useful information about the school. Things like school rules, equipment and uniform information, presentation guidelines, their school timetable and school term dates are all included in them. Quizzing students on this encourages them to review this information and acts as a reminder of the school's expectations.
- **Praise:** Award positive praise using your school's rewards system for planners that are in immaculate condition and are used effectively. This encourages further effective use of them and exemplifies best practice too.
- **Share:** Encourage students to make effective use of their planner by sharing best practice. If you have a visualiser, use this to explore why the planner is so well used. Discuss what it is that is so effective about the way the student is using it. This may sound arduous and to us it is common sense, but embedding effective study habits is and always will be of vital importance to students becoming successful learners. It must be repeated over and over again until they have established healthy study routines.

#planningperfection
#routinesmatter
#learn

Idea 53: Remote learning tips

As we learn to evolve in a new online digital world, we must know the best ways to approach optimal learning experiences for our students.

This idea came about as a result of the recent school closure due to the global coronavirus outbreak. Teachers have very quickly adapted to support the learning needs of their students and we have all become better equipped with skills and knowledge that can be useful for any online learning. Below I share top tips about how to make that learning effective.

- **Be consistent.** Map out the learning fully. Follow a certain structure and format, much like you would in a face-to-face lesson. Students will feel settled and work more effectively if a routine is in place.
- **Avoid text-heavy slides.** These can often make students feel like information overload is occurring and they may switch off entirely.
- **Use live lessons or voice-overs.** These will help students fully understand difficult or challenging topics or concepts.
- **Build in review points.** After each activity, allow some time for students to review what they have learnt. This will help them make progress and build their confidence levels.
- **Set up immediate feedback for quizzing.** In addition to live or recorded lessons, use an online system that allows for immediate feedback for quizzing. For example, if you are a Google school, using Google Forms is a great way to assess how much students have learnt. They get instant feedback and you can check for any gaps in their knowledge and plan to address these in future lessons.
- **Be adaptable.** Be patient and ready to change things if plans don't work out. Online learning is not the same as face-to-face lessons. There are so many other variables at play and it will not always go to plan. Accept that there will be issues and be ready to adapt.
- **Keep things simple.** Overcomplicating things with whizzy PowerPoints or snazzy activities will only convolute the learning. Stick to the simple pattern of: introduce new information, search for meaning, demonstrate understanding, review, reflect and repeat. This will keep students' stress levels in check.

#onlinelearning
#keepitsimple

Chapter 5

Rocking revision

Effective revision strategies both reduce stress and boost confidence for students.

When all the hard work of learning new topics and units is over, there is only one final hurdle before the big exams take place: revision. Often, students will tell me they don't know how to revise. And they'd be correct in telling me this. Their idea of revision is reading through old notes and creating colourful posters. That may seem like they are revising, but in actual fact not much is moving over to the long-term memory as these revision methods are not effective.

This chapter covers a range of ideas to help support students with successful revision. Revision lessons should be as structured as any other lesson in order for students to get as much learning time as possible from them. You will find ideas about different revision methods such as retrieval practice and interleaving, as well as motivational ideas such as revision recovery bags and engaging intervention strategies. Each is designed to ensure students make the most of their revision at what can be the most stressful time during their education. It is important that students feel supported throughout this process with useful learning tools and ideas. Timely, effective revision strategies work to reduce stress levels as students begin to take control of their learning and see gains in their work, which in turn boosts their confidence levels. The end goal of this is happy learners with great exam results.

Idea 54: Revision recovery bags

Showing your students you care works wonders.

This idea came from a wonderful history teacher called Lesley Munro (@LesleyMunro4) and I have since adapted it to suit my own classes. Lesley wanted her students to feel valued and prepared in the weeks running up to external exams.

You'll first need to get yourself some brown paper bags and then find some goodies to fill them with. Lesley included a number of items inside hers:

- **A5 sheets with suggestions for revision strategies:** I usually tell my students to focus on quizzing, mind maps and flashcards as they have repeatedly been shown to be the most successful activities for revision.
- **Exam tips bookmark:** One for each topic or exam paper, which gives a breakdown of what is required for each question, timings and how many marks are available.
- **QR codes bookmark:** Bookmarks with QR codes that take students straight to the revision guides on the school's website and to other useful revision sites.
- **Sticky tabs:** These are used to mark pages in their revision books.
- **A pen:** For obvious reasons.
- **A highlighter:** As above!
- **A little bag of sweets:** To keep them going during the long revision days.
- **A loyalty card:** Students receive a sticker for their card for every revision session or intervention session they attend, for outstanding class work or for outstanding behaviour. They can redeem prizes for a full card.

I add the following items to my own bags:

- **Knowledge organisers:** These are A4 sized and contain everything my students need to know about a text. They're brilliant revision resources. You can find out more about them by reading this blog by Joe Kirby, Deputy Headteacher at Michaela

School: https://pragmaticreform.wordpress.com/2015/03/28/knowledge-organisers.

- **Sticky notes:** I add a load of these to each bag so students can use them for revision.
- **A small note for each student:** You can include words of encouragement for them to reflect on.
- **A party popper:** I allow students to use these at the end of our very last lesson. Again, seeing them smile after all of their hard work is great. It requires a bit of tidying up after!

#connect
#notice

Idea 55: Mind maps

Mind maps are a great, visual way to revise substantial amounts of useful content.

Mind maps have been used in schools for years now, but often students don't know how to create them effectively. I will outline how to create them so that your students get the most beneficial learning from the activity.

What are they?

Mind maps are essentially a visual creation that presents or outlines information on any given topic. They are a great tool for revision.

What are the benefits of mind maps?

- They are a great way to categorise information memorably, rather than simply writing it down in a linear fashion.
- Having all of the required information on one page is helpful for seeing connections between different strands and ideas and, in turn, this aids retention.
- Using colours, codes, images and key information enhances memory retention and is far easier to remember than lots and lots of sentences!
- They allow students to spot connections between ideas that they perhaps wouldn't have spotted if they were simply writing their ideas down separately.
- They can be added to whenever a student remembers something else by simply editing the original map.

How should you make them?

Firstly, start in the middle with the topic you are revising. This will form the central basis from which all other information will stem. Secondly, the branches that stem from the main idea should detail the key themes or strands that connect to the central topic or idea. Finally, from these branches, any other relevant and key ideas should be labelled. It is essentially a spider's web of connected ideas that students need to remember in order to revise successfully for that particular topic. This simple plan should see your students creating effective mind maps in no time.

Are there variations?

Yes. There are many different ways in which you can create mind maps other than simply writing down key ideas in the order described above. Many students choose to use images instead of words that help them to trigger memory. In addition, some students prefer to use symbols and keys to connect their ideas together and help them to retain important information in a more memorable way.

#learning
#memorymindmaps

> **Next steps**
> Why not have students create a mind map at the end of each topic you cover? That way their revision resource will be ready to go.

Idea 56: Apptastic

Apps are a quick and easy way for students to revise.

In the digital age in which we now live, it is important that, as teachers, we know which apps are available for our students to access learning resources at home. The benefit of students using revision apps are that they are easily accessible, can be used at home, contain plenty of quizzes and other formative assessment activities, as well as more formal assessment practice questions. And, let's face it, students love anything digital, so why not put that to good use and encourage them to use revision apps at home?

Here's a selection of revision apps to get them started.

Exam Countdown Lite

This is a simple countdown timer, reminder and test timetable app that both teachers and students can use in order to organise themselves effectively. It enables users to store all exam dates in one place, has an unlimited number of exam countdowns, and uses a colour-coded system for visual organisation. Users can choose from up to 400 icons and have the ability to invite teachers, friends and parents through various social media outlets and via email. It's a great place to start with organising an exam schedule.

Quizlet

Quizlet is a free website and app which provides learning tools for students including flashcards, study and game modes. Students can create their own study sets with key terms and definitions. Students also have the ability to add images to their flashcards for better retention. There are over 40 million user-generated flashcards, so students can search for a topic they are studying and use those too. There are six study and game modes which support students tracking their progress. Flashcards can be shuffled and students can even use audio mode learning. The ability to test and retest is also a useful tool on Quizlet.

Padlet

Padlet is a free app that enables users to create an online bulletin board that they can use to display information from any topic. It's simple to create an account and build a board. Once built, users can add images, links, videos and much more. Users' boards can be shared for collaboration, completely public for anyone to add information or set to private use. The free account allows users to create up to 11 boards at any time. When a board is no longer of any use, simply delete and create a new board. This is a handy tool for shared revision activities.

GCSE Pod

GCSE Pod is an online and app-based learning resource for students. It contains content for over 27 different subjects and over 5,000 podcast-style activities for students to use. The 'Pods' are differentiated by exam board and approved by subject specialists. This app is a quick and easy way for students to test their knowledge on a subject. It's also a great way for teachers to monitor the progress of their students and spot any potential gaps in their learning.

Popplet Lite

Popplet Lite is another great tool for students to use whilst revising. It allows users to enter information and organise it in a visual way to better support retention. Users can capture notes with text, images and even with a drawing tool. This version only allows users to create one Popplet, but there is a feature which allows you to export a completed Popplet and begin a new one.

Adobe Spark Post

This app is a fun way of creating useful revision graphics. Users can get started straight away with a selection of professionally designed templates that can be tweaked to your style. Users simply choose a photo and then add the text to accompany the image. Design filters help to create beautiful, memorable graphics. The app offers a range of layouts, colour palettes, typography styles and filters. Users can also share their creations via social media and email.

Gojimo

Gojimo is a free revision app that contains over 40,000 practice questions. Over 28 different subjects are available at GCSE and 18 at A level, amongst other exam qualifications. Users can download quizzes, track their progress, and strengths and weaknesses, and check off each topic as they revise.

Goji Life also allows users access to information about how to deal with exam pressure and how to manage stress. There are over 70 freely accessible articles that are aimed at preparing students for life.

Next steps
Why not try the apps out for yourself and recommend your favourites to your students?

#apptastic
#revision
#learn

Idea 57: Mnemonic memory

Mnemonics are an easy and efficient way for students to retain and recall key information.

A mnemonic is something very simple that helps you to remember something more challenging. It is usually a system or pattern of letters, associations or ideas. Each letter is a clue to an item that students need to remember. They work because they reduce long phrases to something students can quickly reference. Teachers do this all the time as we simplify our inner complex thoughts in order to share information and understanding with others without confusing them. Another reason mnemonics work is because they are short and brevity is easier to remember than lots of details. The shorter and more distinct they are, the more memorable they are likely to be for our students.

A common example is Richard Of York Gave Battle In Vain. The first letter of each word represents the colours of the rainbow in order: red, orange, yellow, green, blue, indigo and violet. Another typical example could be B.O.D.M.A.S, which is a mathematical mnemonic that stands for brackets, orders, division, multiplication, addition, subtraction. This is the order mathematical calculations should be completed in.

They work particularly well as revision strategies. For example, in English, students may need reminding of some transactional writing techniques that they can use to analyse the tone of someone else's writing or put to use in their own writing. For this, they could remember the mnemonic D.A.F.O.R.E.S.T, which stands for direct address, anecdote, fact, opinion, repetition and rhetorical questions, statistic and triadic structure. This is obviously not an exhaustive list, but it does serve as a prompt that triggers the memory of other writing devices.

Encouraging students to create their own mnemonics, as well as using them with your class, will increase the likelihood of them remembering key information in their exams.

Next steps
Why not have your mnemonics on display in your classroom as a more permanent reminder for your students?

#mnemonicmemory
#learn
#connect

Idea 58: Planning perfection

Effective planning can help students feel confident and fully prepared for their exams.

Share the following revision-planning tips with students:

1. **Create a revision timetable.** Imagine someone trying to train for a marathon without following a training plan. They simply wouldn't be prepared. You need to feel the same way about exam preparation.
2. **Start revising properly in February.** This is not too early but still leaves plenty of time for a range of subjects to be covered.
3. **Revise for smaller amounts of time at the start.** Increase this time gradually as you move towards the exams. Doing too much too soon will cause burnout. A month before the exams begin, revise for up to two hours each night and five to six hours across weekends.
4. **Focus on revising the content of each topic, unit or subject.** Avoid looking at exam questions until you have mastered this.
5. **Don't spend the same amount of time on each subject.** How much time have you already spent revising in lessons? Where are your areas of weakness? Spend more time on these areas to feel confident about all subjects, not just the ones you like.
6. **Be flexible with your timetable.** If the teacher covers something in lesson, change your plan to account for this. Equally, if you are aware of a busy social week ahead, adapt your timetable.
7. **Keep focused.** Focus on one topic at a time. Don't move on until you have grasped it with confidence.
8. **Be 100 per cent sure of the topics and units you must study.** Ask your teachers for a revision list. Use this list to identify your areas of weakness and start there.
9. **Use effective revision strategies.** Ask teachers for advice on flashcards, revision guides, websites, retrieval, spacing and dual coding.
10. **Involve your parents or guardians.** Ask them to quiz you.
11. **When it comes to exam questions, time yourself.** This is so important when you are close to the exams.
12. **Shift your revision focus.** As your exams get closer shift from subject content to exam practice.
13. **Stay calm.** Use effective relaxation strategies to ensure you get enough downtime too.

#planningrevision

Idea 59: Retrieval ready

Spaced out and regular retrieval of knowledge is a tried and tested way for students to retain key exam content.

Three key methods for students to begin revising are spaced retrieval, interleaving and retrieval practice. When combined, they provide a powerful and effective method of revision. Spaced retrieval and retrieval practice are explained below (see Idea 60 for interleaving).

Spaced retrieval

This is a study method that requires students to review and rehearse information. This information is revisited over time, but at different and increasing spaced intervals. The greater the amount of spacing between retrieval events, the greater the potential benefit to retention. It helps students retain access to memorised information over long periods of time because the spacing promotes deeper processing of the learned material. The best results are obtained when the time between learning events is greater than 24 hours and is gradually more spaced out as time goes on. Research has shown that greater retention is still prevalent as long as eight years past the original learning episode when compared to those studying over a concentrated time period.

Retrieval practice

The final method is retrieval practice. This is a method that has been embedded as a non-negotiable task at the start of every lesson in my school. The idea is that topics are recalled rather than simply re-read via exercise and textbooks. It requires students to think hard about what they are being asked to recall. The benefit being that they are more likely to remember it in the future. This method can improve recall performance by as much as 20 per cent.

Next steps

Why not visit the website www.retrievalpractice.com for more information on how you can introduce these methods in your class?

#retrievalready
#learn
#connect

Idea 60: Interleaving

Interleaving is a powerful learning method that ensures successful revision.

For many years, I have been using interleaving as a teaching method and a revision method in my classroom. I came across it in my first teaching post where I used it to plan revision schemes to ensure maximum retention and exam success. Now I also use it to plan learning journeys from topic to topic, ensuring I return to prior learnt information as often as I can. For those who are unfamiliar with it, interleaving involves switching between different topics and ideas so that long-term learning can take place. It has been proven to work better than teaching units of work or topics in blocks.

A German psychologist named Hermann Ebbinghaus studied how the memory works and designed the 'forgetting curve'. This shows how newly learned information can be forgotten over time if there is no attempt to retain it. It is a useful planning tool when it comes to revision timetables and structure, as it increases the chances of students retaining and remembering information.

It is important to note that the topics being interleaved must have some connection or the learning that takes place isn't as well remembered. A well-designed revision schedule will take account of this. It helps students to see links, similarities and differences between topics more clearly. Here are two more revision ideas to think about.

In my experience, revision lessons should not be lessons that are unstructured with little support. Students need guidance and motivation when it comes to revision. Otherwise, there is a temptation simply to create endless amounts of notes or posters that may offer them a sense of satisfaction but, in terms of memory retention, do very little. By interleaving your revision lessons, you are securing the best possible chance of the students being successful in their exams.

You may also want to suggest that the students themselves practise interleaving in their own revision timetables. This will make doubly sure that their retention and storage of information are long term.

#interleaving
#connect

Idea 61: Dual coding

Dual coding is an effective way of storing information whilst revising.

Dual coding is a process in which verbal or written materials are accompanied by visual materials. The idea is that you present students with information in two connected formats, which gives students a greater chance of remembering the information at a later date. The visuals can be anything from graphs, timelines, images, infographics, cartoon strips, symbols and so on.

How can students use this method?

When students are creating their revision materials, ask them to assign dual coding to each element of their study. It doesn't matter what it is, as long as each visual represents the learning point in some way. Encourage students to ask themselves, 'What do these visuals tell me about the learning point?' and 'What does the learning point tell me about the visual?' If they cannot recall the information via both methods, they may need to choose better visuals. It is worth noting that some visuals work better than others with certain topics. When revising time periods, for example, visuals such as timelines are better. Remembering the different stages of a narrative is best paired with a diagram of each stage.

Once they have set out their revision materials with both text and visual attached, they can begin to revise. Ask them to look at only the visuals and recall the text information by writing their ideas down. Ask them to look at the text information only and recall the visuals by drawing them out. This should be repeated using spaced retrieval and retrieval practice methods (see Idea 59: Retrieval ready on page 103 for information on these). It doesn't matter if the information is not exactly the same as the original material, as long as it is all covered in some way. By the end of the revision season, students should be able to recall knowledge confidently using this method.

Next steps

Check out Oliver Caviglioli's website (www.olicav.com) all about dual coding, where you can find much more information on the power of visuals, as well as a book aimed at teachers about dual coding in particular: *Dual Coding With Teachers*.

#dualcoding
#connect
#learn

Idea 62: Chanting for success

Chanting is an effective way to remember key information during revision season.

Revision chants have been designed to support students in either their retention and recall, or their motivation and resilience. Claire Thompson, assistant headteacher at Whitefield School, North London, writes about how she uses this idea in her lessons.

How they work

First, think of the reason for a chant. I find the most effective chants are those used to address misconceptions, to embed structures for answering exam questions, or as a motivator.

For example, when addressing a misconception, the following chant could be used:

'I will not use apostrophes to indicate plurals.'

An example for addressing exam skills, in this case imaginative writing structure, would be:

'Setting, shift, zoom in, zoom out.'

Finally, a chant that can be used as a motivator for success is:

'Rain hard; fight easy!'

Once you have chosen the chant, you must establish it with the students. There are a number of ways that you can do this, but modelling the chant first is essential. I find the two most effective ways are to ask students to repeat what you have said or to make associations with key triggers.

For example:

Say it with me, 'I must use a topic sentence to introduce a paragraph.'

'When I say "repetition", you say "emphasis"'

Don't worry if you are a little unsure about beginning the chanting activity. Start small and use one or two words as practice. It's amazing how quickly the students get on board and the atmosphere in the room becomes exciting yet purposeful. Before you know it, you'll have many classes happily chanting for success and dare I say it, you might even enjoy it yourself!

Next steps

Interleave chants throughout your lessons during the year, but frequently during revision season to build students' confidence and motivate them to do well.

- Use chants as exit tickets at the end of your lesson. That way, there is absolute buy-in at all times.
- Use chants as part of a competition: which side of the room can say it the loudest? This will really get them going with their regular chanting. Who doesn't love competition?
- Introduce clapping to match the rhythm. This is not only effective, but enjoyable too.

Why not give chanting for success a go in your classroom? Create your mantras and get chanting!

#chantingforsuccess
#connect

Idea 63: Effective elaboration

Encouraging students to elaborate on their ideas is an effective revision method that builds knowledge over time.

Rebeka Aylwin, sociology teacher and head of the humanities faculty at Oriel High School in Crawley, shares how she encourages her students to elaborate.

A common barrier to effective revision for many students is that they don't know what they don't know. Encouraging students to assess their knowledge and understanding through testing themselves can take a range of formats. Elaboration is a great starting point for students to highlight their areas of strength, and also move out of their revision comfort zone, to focus on their areas of weakness.

Students should begin with their notes to hand. Having prompts to form the foundation of their revision session ensures they have a starting block to build upon, which helps to break the intimidation of a blank page. Remembering that practice doesn't just make perfect, but it also makes permanent; students must use their notes to make sure they are remembering the correct information.

Prompts give the bare bones from which to start their elaboration and should be broken down into small and manageable chunks of information. Some effective prompts include:

- key vocabulary mats
- diagrams or graphs
- illustrations
- a copy of the syllabus
- personalised learning checklists
- topic sentences
- exam questions.

From this point, there are a number of ways you can use elaboration to build knowledge and understanding.

Step 1

A simple way to begin is with a 'brain dump'. Using the prompts, students list or mind map anything they can remember about a particular topic, in no specific order. This uncomplicated strategy means they can just focus on getting their ideas on paper and that this information can be developed with further elaboration activities. At this point I encourage students to check their notes, make corrections and add anything they've left out. Using a different-coloured pen to do so can help highlight the parts that are more of a challenge to remember. Doing this activity a few times should help to improve recall until they are able to retain the majority of the information on a topic.

Step 2

Urge students to go beyond recall, deepening their understanding of the topic by asking questions, and lots of them. Giving them a list of question stems that escalate in difficulty can ensure the information they revise is digested using their higher-order thinking skills. This could be done independently as a written activity, or verbally as a paired activity. For example:

- Who was…?
- What are the features of…?
- Why did X happen?
- When did…?
- What caused…?
- How can you explain…?
- What happens when…?
- What could be different if…?
- What changes would you make to solve…?
- Can you predict the outcome if…?

Step 3

Students can develop their elaboration activities further by building connections between ideas on the same topic. One way to do this is to get them to randomly pick two ideas from their prompt list and draw a table with the headings 'similarities' and 'differences'. The advice given on how to do this will be very context bound, but students can be encouraged to think of all the factors that these ideas, concepts, theories or events have in common with each other, and what makes them stand out. The more students can add connections and details, the deeper their learning.

Step 4

Another way of making connections is through our own experiences, either through past memory or day-to-day life. Prior learning and encounters can teach students categories and concrete examples, which can provide the glue for understanding and in-depth learning. Getting students to make associations between information in their short-term working memory and information that is already in their long-term memory can help to create 'hooks'. These hooks help to strengthen connections in their memory, organise ideas, produce explanations and bring information to the front of their minds more easily. Encourage students to think about when they may have experienced something similar and where they may see what they are learning in real life. You can also guide students to make these connections by modelling concrete examples in your own life. By doing this, students are essentially connecting newer information to embedded knowledge and integrating new material into their long-term memory.

Once students are confident practitioners in elaboration, they should work their way towards revising without their prompt material, whilst also remembering to check their information in their class notes or with their teacher. Ensure that students do not over-complicate their elaborations but use them instead to build connections between information to strengthen the pathways in their memories. Elaboration can be a challenging revision activity as it requires us to think about information in a range of different ways. One reminder I always give my students at this point is that the bits where they really struggle are also the ones where they are learning the most.

#elaborationeffective
#connectthelearning
#learn

Idea 64: Blank knowledge organisers

Filling in blank knowledge organisers ensures students know which areas to focus on in revision before they begin.

Laura May Rowlands, head of faculty for English and Literacy at Woodlands Community College in Southampton, shares how she uses this idea in her classroom.

One way to reduce stress for students in the run-up to the exams is to get them to check what they do and don't know. Enter: the blank knowledge organiser. This is a great way of checking what students don't need to spend more time on and what they do need to focus on. Ask students to undertake this activity weekly during the revision season for maximum impact.

What to do

Ask students to look at their populated knowledge organiser. It should be grouped into several columns with headings as set out by the teacher (see Idea 43 on page 68). Ask students to recreate the outline on a blank piece of paper. They have five minutes to try and 'populate' the boxes with as much information as they remember. If they need to, they can leave some blank – their first clue about what has made it into their long-term memory.

Next, this is the step which may hurt their pride. Ask students to use a different-coloured pen. Using your original knowledge organiser, tell them to fill in the blank sections. Let's say they used black pen at first and then filled in the blanks with a green pen. The black-pen work is all of the knowledge they have secured in their long-term memory – it's important to ask students to revisit this as part of their revision, but this isn't what needs work. The section in green pen should be their focus for that week. This process should be repeated weekly until all of the knowledge from the populated knowledge organiser has been secured.

#blankorganisers
#learn

Idea 65: Booklet sense

Using booklets for different topics is an effective tried and tested revision method.

Laura Tsabet, English teacher and Director of CPD and ITT at Avonbourne Academies, Bournemouth, shares how she uses revision booklets in her class.

Booklets (resources that contain all knowledge to be taught plus space for students to do their work) have slowly but surely gained popularity over recent years, particularly for use in lessons where there is lots of resource-heavy content, or even in cases where there may be non-subject specialists delivering lessons. They can be great for alerting students to the sequence of lessons they are going to study and for keeping things all in one place.

But actually, booklets can be fabulous tools for revision too – whether that is designing lesson booklets with the intent that they one day serve as revision, or creating entire booklets dedicated for this sole purpose. Arguably, the best revision booklets are those created with this specific purpose in mind. They differ from booklets used in lessons as they are less content heavy and more about recalling and retrieving the information students have been taught, or practising exam responses.

In order to ensure that students know what they need to revise, teachers should provide a list of the things that they need to cover. This should preferably be in an order that is relevant to them – chronological, alphabetical or in the same order it was covered in lessons. A simple way for students to identify what they should prioritise is to provide space for them to rate themselves against the list, either by numbering their confidence from 1 to 5, or rating themselves against a set of traffic lights or emojis. Teachers can check students' confidence by intermittently self-assessing them against the same criteria in lessons, providing timely interventions for struggling students and thereby monitoring wellbeing.

It can be daunting for students to approach revision when they are essentially testing their own memories, so having a carefully placed knowledge organiser in the front of the booklet is useful for them to check their answers. Knowledge organisers are an excellent resource for improving student wellbeing; many students enjoy the feeling that they are clever and being able to recall accurate information can give them this feeling of success. It is important to note, though, that any knowledge organiser used within revision booklets should be one that students are already familiar with – perhaps used in lessons throughout the unit – so that they are not unnecessarily flustered by different layouts or prioritised information (see Idea 43 on page 68).

Having a range of well-written models is also key to an effective revision booklet. What a good answer looks like is often something that students fret over again and again. When they're revising at home, this is impossible for teachers to manage, so providing answers from each band of the mark scheme in booklets is advised; it effectively gives students something concrete to compare their own practice responses with and can reduce these anxieties. Additionally, one of the joys of booklets is that they are created on computers so models can be colour coded against the mark scheme, or any acronyms used in lessons, and students can replicate this coding when checking their own answers.

With this in mind, when it comes to student wellbeing, we must be careful about how we approach revision. It can feel particularly stressful for students to be handed piles of paper, revision guides and textbooks, only to be told, 'Now revise.' Often, it won't be immediately obvious how many of the resources will actually be useful for them; they may not know how to use these resources without explicitly being taught.

The same goes for booklets. Many well-meaning teachers design revision booklets for their classes – particularly for GCSE – and share them online for free. Whilst this should never be discouraged (these people are absolute heroes in my eyes), we should be careful with these resources. Many teachers have different styles and different ways of teaching things and so it can actually be detrimental for students' wellbeing to be given booklets which contain a different way of doing things to what they have learnt in class. Whilst it may seem obvious to many professionals that the stuff in the booklets is essentially the same, even minor discrepancies can cause confusion and panic amongst students. What this means is teachers should adapt the booklets to suit their own classes before passing them out for revision, checking any acronyms used or models for disparity with their own. That way, students are happier with the revision and any unnecessary stress or burden is removed.

#revisionbooklets

Chapter 6

Super citizens

Ensuring students are ready for the next steps in their journey means ensuring they are well-rounded, helpful citizens.

As educators, our role isn't just to teach the content of our subject and that's the end of it. We are in one of the most privileged positions there is in society. We are lucky enough to be able to shape hundreds of young minds every single year. It is our moral duty to ensure they are well-rounded, socially responsible citizens as well as excellent learners.

This chapter focuses on the idea of students being great citizens. It contains ideas to encourage young people to be more outgoing and resilient and to make a positive contribution to society. A sense of belonging is important for all individuals in society, as it encourages people to be more supportive and considerate of the society in which they live. If students immerse themselves in society by making a positive contribution, they will feel that sense of belonging and that will, in turn, lead to feelings of self-worth and value as an individual. You will find ideas about schemes such as The Duke of Edinburgh's Award, National Citizens Service and volunteer schemes as well as more general advice about how to get students thinking about widening their connection with the community, such as the Postcards of Kindness scheme. Enjoy reading through them and think about which ideas would be most useful in your school.

Idea 66: Student leadership

Student leadership roles encourage responsibility and independence.

Students develop as young people when we give them responsibility. This builds trust between you and your students, as well as making your life a little easier. There are many ways to do this as a school but you can encourage student leadership in class too. When students become leaders, they are outside of their comfort zone. Once they are successful at leadership, their confidence grows and they feel good about achievements, less fearful of new experiences and generally happier.

- **Assign roles.** Stephen Lockyer has this idea nailed with his wonderful invention, the class job wheel. On the wheel is a list of jobs, together with the class list, which means that jobs are rotated each week and, over the year, every student will have done each job.
- **When students begin in your class each year, assign them numbers.** At the beginning and end of the lesson, for example, you could ask the '2s' to distribute or collect in the exercise books. This is rotated across all groups evenly. (Students can also stay in these numbers for group work, which allows for a quick start for tasks.)
- **As a form tutor, roles can also be distributed across your tutees.** Have someone responsible for collecting the reading books. Allow some to take care of classroom displays, shelves or plants. Rotate these roles throughout the year using the job wheel.
- **Nominate class reading leaders.** Pair up stronger readers with less confident readers. This has the added benefit of developing relationships between students too.
- **Choose some students to be homework leaders.** Allow them to help others with homework when they are stuck or struggling. Again, this supports relationships and independence.
- **Appoint table or group leaders and encourage them to take a leading role in activities.** The experience of leading their peers will develop their confidence and communication skills.

Next steps

Why not volunteer to run a whole-school student leadership programme? You can link it to the pastoral curriculum.

#leaders
#volunteer
#connect

Idea 67: National Citizens Service

Encouraging students to become involved in supporting the wider society shapes their future and develops social responsibility.

The National Citizens Service is a personal and social development programme aimed at 15- to 17-year-olds in the UK. It was set up in 2011 and, due to its success, was made permanent by the National Citizens Service Act 2017. Its aim is to encourage, challenge and develop young people into confident, socially aware young adults. It's totally voluntary and takes place during school holidays, so it's perfect for keeping young people busy in a positive way. The service is split into four phases.

- **Phase one:** A residential visit to an outdoor education centre. This phase involves physical and team-building activities. A great phase for students who have never left their home town.
- **Phase two:** Another residential phase: this time students have the chance to live independently. They are taught important life skills. This can be hugely beneficial for the students who don't necessarily get this type of advice at home.
- **Phase three and four:** The social project phase. Here students work together to plan and deliver a social action project in their local community. This might involve raising awareness of a particular social issue or fundraising for a particular cause. This final phase really encourages students to be socially responsible young people.

The service is largely funded by the government and as a result the charge for each student is only £50. There are also bursaries available for those who cannot afford the fee.

Of the students I know who have undertaken the challenge, all have come back with nothing but positive things to say about it. I also noticed a real difference in their levels of confidence and maturity. It was clear that their wellbeing had been positively affected by their experiences.

#nationalcitizensservice
#doyourduty

Idea 68: Beyond the classroom

Extra-curricular activities develop positive relationships with students and promote wellbeing.

One of the best ways to build positive relationships with your students is to get to know them beyond the confined space of your classroom. Over the years, I have taken part in many extra-curricular activities. I have found time and time again that the relationships I have with the students I teach have been made stronger by doing so. Getting to know students in this way encourages them to be confident learners too, as they naturally become more comfortable with you. Here are some of the ways in which you can get involved.

School trips

Trips are a great way to get students involved in your subject or a topic you are teaching. I have taken students to the Houses of Parliament and the Old Bailey as part of their law course, and visited the Somme Battlefields and read war poetry from the exact spot it was written during the First World War. I have also taken part in Year 7 adventure trips to the Ardèche region in France, and visited the theatre many times with my English literature students. What better way to promote your subject and ensure students are enjoying themselves? Why not think about a trip that you could help out on?

Clubs

Why not set up a club for students in your school? Of course, if you wish, it can be relevant to your subject. For example, the Key Stage 3 coordinator at my school, Aanisah Khan, runs the Leaders in English club – but it doesn't have to be subject specific. I know teachers who have set up choirs, baking clubs and gaming clubs. The benefits are clear; students are engaging in activities beyond the classroom and this creates a healthy balance of work and play. Why not set up a club or attend a current club to develop your relationship with your students?

Competitions

Whether they be whole-school or just little competitions within your area, these are great for engaging students and encouraging participation. Students develop a sense of pride in their work which makes them feel good about themselves. In the past, I have run literacy competitions, house competitions, and even competitions to raise money for charities. What could you create in your school to promote student wellbeing?

#extrateacher
#volunteer
#learn

Next steps

Before you set up your own trip, club or competition, it might be a good idea to find out what your school already offers. Is there a space for what you would like to set up? It might also be worth attending an extra-curricular event at your school to see how things work before you decide what type of activity you would like to promote.

Idea 69: The Duke of Edinburgh's Award

Encouraging students to get out and about in the community does wonders for their wellbeing.

The Duke of Edinburgh's Award was set up by Prince Philip in 1956. It is now recognised in 144 nations across the world. It encourages young people aged 14 to 24 to get outside and work on a series of self-improvement exercises. Young people are then awarded either a bronze, silver or gold award. These awards are recognised by employers as a mark of good character. Other benefits include: improved socialisation skills, better health and wellbeing, stronger self-esteem and confidence, and a love of the great outdoors! There are four sections in each award and a fifth in the gold award:

- **Physical section:** This is the requirement to keep fit. Young people can choose any sport, dance or fitness activity.
- **Skills section:** The requirement for young people to develop a particular skill in a new hobby or activity. Young people must show that they have broadened their knowledge and that their expertise has grown as a result. Examples include learning the skill of coaching a football team or learning how to care for an animal.
- **Volunteering section:** Volunteering could involve helping people, the community, the environment or animals. It encourages social responsibility and ensures teenagers grow into responsible adults.
- **Expedition section:** This involves planning, training for and undertaking a completely self-reliant expedition. This section promotes independence and confidence in young people as well as improving their navigational skills. Many young people choose to go hiking, learning about key mapping and coordinate skills along the way.
- **Residential section:** Young people go on a residential in a group of five or more and undertake team-building activities. This section promotes independence and confidence as they are not permitted to go with friends. It's a great way to develop mature young adults.

Next steps

Does your school offer The Duke of Edinburgh's Award? If not, why not look into running it yourself?

#dukeofedinburgh
#exercise

Idea 70: Postcards of Kindness

Sending postcards shows you care.

The Postcards of Kindness scheme was set up by care home provider Your Health Group. In 2018, a campaign was launched asking members of the public to send their residents postcards. In 2019, they decided to make this a bigger campaign and invited other care homes to become involved. Their aim was simple: to combat loneliness and isolation across the country. Many schools now use the scheme to set up links with care homes and encourage young people to write. This is a great idea that your students can become involved with on a regular basis.

How to get involved?

Firstly, join the Facebook group: Postcards of Kindness. Secondly, click on the 'Files' tab at the top of the group page to find a list of care home addresses; a PowerPoint to deliver to your class; a document explaining how to use the spreadsheet; and finally, some ideas to encourage your students to write. You will also find a tab for the 100 Club here. This is a list of all the residents who are turning 100 or older each month! What a great idea for students to send them a birthday card.

Why do it?

The divide between the young and the old is vast. Many young people spend very little time with the elderly. What better way to try and connect two very different generations? It offers students the opportunity to be creative. My students designed and wrote their own postcards, for example. The actual act of sending the cards is very rewarding for the students. They genuinely feel a sense of pride in what they are doing. Equally, the prospect of a reply fills them with excitement. It's also wonderful to see images of the residents with their postcards (these are shared on the Facebook group). Why not give it a go with your class?

Next steps
One class not enough? Ask the heads of year if it can be rolled out across the school!

#postcardsofkindness
#connect
#volunteer

Idea 71: Senior citizens' party

Inviting the local community into school for a party encourages students' community spirit.

One of the highlights of my school year is when my school invites the local senior citizens to school for their annual Christmas party. Spending time with older members of society develops students' communication skills, not to mention their empathy. All too often in the sensationalist media, young people are castigated for their various wrongdoings. This presents them in a bad light to older generations. Affording the elderly the opportunity to see just how wonderful young people are goes some way to correcting this negative image.

How does it work?

Firstly, someone needs to take the lead on the organisation of the event. Once this is decided, the following steps may be of use.

- Set a date early and ensure it is placed on the school calendar.
- Get together an organisational student group (this could be part of a hospitality course).
- Contact local care homes inviting them to the event. Invites could be designed by art students or during form time.
- Ask staff to donate food and gifts for the elderly so that each resident receives a small Christmas parcel to take home with them.
- Liaise with the catering teacher and the staff catering team. Organise for catering students to be responsible for preparing some of the food and for serving the food on the day.
- Ensure the student group have organised volunteer helpers for the day of the event, decorations and some entertainment too. They could enlist the help of the music and drama departments.
- Enlist staff to volunteer on the day of the event by driving residents to and from their homes, as well as offering general support.

This is a substantial and lengthy feat, but the reward is truly heartwarming. Watching the students interact with the elderly in such a supportive way and seeing the joy on the residents' faces is simply wonderful.

#seniorcitizensday

Idea 72: Valiant volunteers

Volunteering leaves students feeling better connected to society and socialisation can work to reduce stress and anxiety levels.

There are many ways in which young people can volunteer in our communities and the benefits are many. The prospect of volunteering may seem daunting to a young person but why not explore the benefits with them and see how they get on? Benefits include:

- Volunteering connects young people to people they would not normally meet in the community and helps make it a better place.
- Young people receive the benefit of making new friends, expanding their network and boosting their social skills. Volunteering also has the added benefit of being good for your body and mind. Researchers have proven time and again that giving to others makes us feel good. Humans are hard-wired to be generous. The more we give, the happier we feel and volunteering is a great way to do so.
- Depending on the type of volunteering young people take part in, there is the added benefit of stress and anxiety reduction. Working with animals is known to reduce stress, for example.
- Young people will feel a boost in confidence as they support others in need, as well as feeling a real sense of purpose in their work.
- Volunteering looks great on a young person's curriculum vitae. It teaches young people valuable job skills and instils a sense of responsibility that could prove valuable when it comes to employment.
- Volunteering allows young people to gain valuable career experience and brings a sense of fun and enjoyment to young people as they try out new skills and experiences.
- If they choose their volunteering role well, it can provide renewed creativity, passion and drive. Young people are left feeling like they have made a real difference to the lives of those in need, while also feeling a sense of accomplishment in the development of their own skills.

What's not to love? Why not introduce the idea of volunteering to the young people in your school?

#volunteerwork

Idea 73: Volunteer schemes

So, how do students volunteer? There are many ways in which this can be done.

Here are a few ideas of volunteer schemes to get students started.

Local charity shops

Charity shops rely on the good will of local people to support the running of their stores. They are often looking for volunteers to help run the shop floor and sort and organise their stock. It is worth visiting them to see if they have any volunteer positions available. This is also a great way for young people to learn about the importance of giving and generosity as they will come into contact with this from the minute they enter the shop.

Local animal charities and sanctuaries

Animal shelters often take on young volunteers to help care for the animals in their charge. A young person interested in this work could find themselves walking the dogs, on feeding duties or cleaning out the pens, for example. Why not take a look at what's available in your school's local area?

Local care homes

Care homes are also great places to volunteer. Often their residents don't receive any visitors at all. It's a great opportunity for young people to meet people from a different generation to their own and make some new friends, whilst also offering the support of friendship to those who need it most.

Local businesses

There are lots of volunteering opportunities available at local businesses too. Summer schemes are available for those looking for experience in a particular field of work and it is worth checking with local companies to see what they offer for young people.

These are just a few of the places in which young people could look for volunteering opportunities. I would stress that young people should always go accompanied by an adult to ensure that the volunteer work they are doing is properly organised and that parents are aware of their role.

Next steps

Why not take your volunteering to the next level by taking part in something like World Challenge? World Challenge offers volunteering opportunities of a different kind. They offer overseas travel experiences that develop young people into global citizens and offer fantastic learning opportunities that simply couldn't be experienced otherwise. Trips that students in my previous school had been on included one to Tanzania to help build a local school, and more recently to Malaysia to volunteer at a local turtle sanctuary.

#volunteerwork
#connect
#learn
#notice

Idea 74: Part-time jobs

A great way for young people to begin connecting with their local community is by taking up a part-time job.

Students often mention that they become easily bored at home. When exam season isn't in full swing, they can find it difficult to occupy their time with worthwhile activities, and I'm not talking about mindlessly scrolling through YouTube videos or spending hours on end on games consoles here. A part-time job can offer them a break from this boredom and instil in them a sense of responsibility. As a young teen myself, I delivered papers around the village I grew up in. It made me understand the importance of punctuality and it certainly got me out of bed on time! The kind of roles students can take up are limited and there are legal requirements that must be abided by. The following information documents the law regarding working rules for young people and the type of role they could look for.

The legal requirements

14 is considered the minimum age that a young person can begin a part-time job. At this age, the type of work a young person can do is defined as 'light work'. They are not allowed to do any job that may affect their health and safety or interfere with their education. In terms of the hours they are allowed to work the following applies:

- During school time, a maximum of 12 hours per week is acceptable. These hours must be worked within the parameters of two hours on school days and Sundays and up to six hours on Saturdays.
- During the school holidays the hours change to a maximum of 25 per week: five on weekdays and Saturdays and two on Sundays.

For 15- and 16-year-olds still in full-time education, the following applies:

- A maximum of 12 hours per week, with two hours on weekdays and Sundays and up to eight hours on Saturdays.
- During the holidays, this changes to 35 hours per week: eight hours during weekdays and Saturdays and two hours on Sundays.

Young people aged 14 to 16 cannot work outside of the hours of 7am and 7pm, they must have a two-week break from work each year and they must have a one-hour rest break for every four hours they work.

Once students leave full-time education, they may begin working full-time hours. This begins from the last Friday in June after their 16th birthday. As you probably know, there is a requirement for all young people to remain in some form of education until they reach the age of 18. They may work during this time as long as they cover 280 guided learning hours each year. By informing students of the laws around part-time jobs, you are keeping them safe and their rights protected.

What type of jobs can young people hold?

Those over 14 years of age looking for work can expect to be doing one of the roles listed below:

- delivering newspapers and leaflets
- babysitting
- dog walking and pet sitting
- car washing
- gardening jobs
- shop work, including stacking shelves
- work in an office
- work in a hairdressers
- work in a cafe or restaurant, excluding the kitchen
- work in hotels or other places offering accommodation.

Ask students to check their local community for existing jobs that they wish to undertake. Often, a great place to check is the advertisement space in newsagents' shop windows.

Those over 16 years of age have a wider variety of roles available to them. Some of them are listed below:

- Bar or restaurant jobs. Legal requirements exist here too. For example, you must be 16 or 17 to be able to serve alcohol and that is only when it is being drunk with a meal. This is usually when being observed or approved by an older bar staff member.
- Shop jobs. Work in supermarkets for teenagers is aimed at those aged 16 or over and usually involves stacking shelves.

- Online jobs for those over 16 years but not yet 18 years. Some examples include: typing jobs, test driving websites, translation jobs, data entry work, proofreading and so on.
- Online paid surveys also occasionally target their demographic at teenagers.
- Lifeguards can train at age 16, so this is also a possibility.
- Sports coaching can also be undertaken at age 16 and training qualifications are available.

Again, advising young people about where to look will support them in seeking out part-time work. The internet is a vast place for them to research on their own. Ensure you are offering the right advice when it comes to part-time jobs.

Next steps
Why not set up a display in your tutor room about the laws regarding part-time work and the type of job your students could undertake?

#parttimejobs
#responsibility
#connect

Idea 75: The wonder of work experience

Work experience for students supports local businesses whilst developing students' skills.

In England, the current law states that young people must stay in education until they are 18. This changed from age 16 in 2008. Since then, more and more schools have decided to take away the opportunity for students to undergo work experience in the local community. This, of course, was also brought about, in part, by the recent GCSE overhaul, which placed time constraints on teachers in terms of delivering the content required for the new exams. As a result of this, bonds that were perhaps strong between local businesses and schools have weakened and students are not being offered the chance to develop their skills in a profession of interest.

This is a disappointing trend, as students found work experience to be valuable. Many would decide on their chosen career path on the basis of these experiences. As a 16-year-old, I myself went to a primary school to do work experience. I still remember it to this day. The act of being treated like an adult, coupled with the sense of responsibility I felt, was a powerful determiner of my future and, after a few about turns, here I am as a teacher.

If schools are serious about supporting their students and developing them as adults, they should continue to run work experience weeks for them. What other opportunity provides them with such a fully immersive experience? When else will students get the opportunity to experience a job before they are actually doing it? Never, in most cases. Not only that, it helps to develop strong links with local businesses. These businesses may, in turn, support the school when they need it, for example at charity events.

#workexperiencesurvival
#connect
#learn

Idea 76: Charity champions

Raising money for charity encourages community spirit amongst pupils.

This idea is pretty much a given in all schools. All of the schools I've worked in have, at some point, raised money for charity, whether it be a small cake sale or a much grander event such as a charity concert. I was lucky enough to work in one school where charity fundraising was at the heart of the pastoral house system. As a head of house, I was given the opportunity to choose a charity to be affiliated with my house. I chose a local children's hospice. I'll never forget the feeling of being able to raise a significant amount of money for such a worthy cause. At my current school, I am regularly enlisting the support of students to fundraise for various charities. By role modelling this type of charitable behaviour, students are learning themselves to be better conscientious citizens who do what they can to support those less fortunate than themselves.

If your school isn't already raising money for charity, consider some of the ideas below:

- **Formalise the fundraising:** Attach charities to the pastoral curriculum through the house or college system in your school. Make a competition out of it to see which tutor groups and houses make the most for their chosen charity.
- **Cake sales:** Why not allow students the opportunity to raise money for charity in this way? Macmillan Coffee Morning is a good place to start.
- **Sponsored events:** These can be held on celebration days or at the end of the year to raise money for local charities.
- **Awareness days:** Charities like Comic Relief, Children in Need and Save the Children all rely heavily on schools taking part in their events and students love the red noses, spotty clothing and Christmas jumper days too.
- **Support local charities:** Find out what local charities there are in your area and see if you can raise funds for them. They rely on their local community to support their cause much more than the larger charities and are working on shoestring budgets to do incredible things.

#charitymatters
#volunteer

Idea 77: Student exchange

Exchanges allow young people to experience life in another country.

One of the many things I never got to do as a young person myself was go on the student exchange programme at secondary school. It was always a huge regret of mine as those who did go seemed to have nothing but positive experiences to share about the time they spent abroad. There are many advantages of a student exchange programme:

- International learning encourages acceptance and an understanding of different cultures and community perspectives.
- Students have the opportunity to learn a language by immersion.
- Being in another country challenges students' problem-solving skills.
- It builds skills such as confidence, self-esteem and independence.
- It develops students' maturity as they learn how to behave in social situations without the support of their family and friends.
- Prospective employers look favourably on students who have spent time abroad immersing themselves into life in another country.
- Students demonstrate many skills such as successfully learning compromise and flexibility in challenging circumstances.
- It often results in long-term friendships that go on to develop into adulthood and later life, further reinforcing stronger cultural ties between countries. We could all do with a little more of that!

How to get started

- Find a reputable company to set up the student exchange. Seek advice from local schools who offer exchanges.
- Think about how to make connections before the trip. Pair families up and ask students to write letters to their exchange family. Take part in Skype conversations to ensure each student feels comfortable with the family before they leave. Agree activities for students to do whilst away.
- Stay in touch whilst they are away so no student feels isolated. Most of all, have fun. It's a fantastic opportunity.

#studentexchange

Idea 78: Community spirit

Encouraging participation in school events develops students' community spirit.

One of the best ways to ensure students understand the importance of community is to get them on board in the small community they are part of every single day. Every school needs its student champions. It is often too easy for students to breeze through school without ever having supported their little part of the world in any way. If left unnoticed, this can lead to an overriding sense of self-involved individual responsibility and not much community spirit. I'm sure you'll all agree – this isn't what we want for our lovely students. In the words of J. B. Priestley, 'We are all responsible for each other. We are members of one body.' We want our youngsters to leave school successful, no doubt about that. And that success includes them leaving with a collective sense of social responsibility. So, what can we do to encourage more of this attitude in school? Here are some ideas.

The school show

The big annual event! Every school has one. The time, organisation and patience needed by staff to ensure this event runs smoothly is exceptional. It takes months of planning and a considerable amount of cajoling in some cases to get students on board. But once the show arrives, it becomes clear that the whole effort was entirely worth it. This event is a great opportunity for students to get involved in wider school life. They don't have to be a talented singer or dancer to take part either. At my school, aside from the main stage roles, there are a number of roles off stage that need filling. It's a huge event that involves: catering support, stage creation support, technical stage support, front of house support, audience care support and more. Any student I have ever spoken to about taking part has never regretted being involved.

Subject leaders

This is an opportunity for students to lead in areas that they really enjoy. Responsibilities might include planning and organising trips; helping in the subject's office or store room; planning and taking surveys and analysing the results; helping out in after-school clubs and supporting any competitions that are run. It's a really useful activity to add to any CV too, especially if you wish to take the subject at university.

Charity fundraising

Every school I have ever worked at has had a named charity whom they fundraise for each year. It works differently in each school, of course. My first school had charities assigned to each house. My current school changes their charity each year. However it operates in your school, it is a perfect example of how students can become involved in another community event. The possibilities are endless. They could hold bake sales, plan quiz nights, organise non-uniform events and partake in various other competitions to raise money for their chosen charity.

Assemblies

A great way to get students out of their comfort zones and thrust into the limelight is to have them plan and deliver assemblies. In my school, each form in each year group is given one assembly slot per year to present on something they feel is important to them. This is a real group effort and it's fantastic to see how well groups communicate and deliver important messages to their peers.

External competitions

These are the perfect addition to any school as they allow students to represent their place of study at a local and national level. Competitions such as those presented by the Jack Petchey Foundation (see here: www.jackpetcheyfoundation.org.uk), Poetry Live (see here: http://poetrylive.net) and Smart Law's Mock Magistrate Trial (see here: https://smartlaw.org.uk/mock-trials) are not only lots of fun, but they also allow students some freedom of expression and time away from the grindstone that is their daily study. It also allows the school to develop its reputation as a great school across local and national arenas.

This isn't an exhaustive list and I'd love to know what happens in your school to encourage more community-minded young people. Why not share your community fun and photos online using the hashtags below? (Just don't forget to seek permission before any images are shared.)

#schoolchampions
#connect

Next steps
Consider what is available in your own school. What other opportunities could be set up?

Chapter 7

Whole-school student wellbeing

A whole-school overview of student wellbeing is an important aspect of any school.

In every school, there are islands of success, pockets of wisdom and innovative educators who really do have the best relationships with the students they serve and achieve great results with them too, but in order to get the most out of our students at a whole-school level, there must be a consistent and practical approach to their wellbeing that all staff members both understand and buy in to. Schools operate best when everyone works together in order for young people to succeed.

This chapter covers a range of ideas worthy of consideration by any senior leadership team. Areas such as the curriculum, student surveys, mentoring systems and rewards are covered. It also includes ideas about specific roles that staff could hold within a school, such as an equality and inclusivity lead or wellbeing lead, in order to keep students' wellbeing a primary focus at all times. Take a look and see what ideas could be of use in your school setting.

Idea 79: Curriculum care

A well thought out, appropriate curriculum ensures students' learning is meaningful.

This idea includes a summary of the finer details of Ofsted's new curriculum framework guidance. It should be no surprise to anyone in education that curriculum is the new buzzword right now. With Ofsted's new framework already securely embedded, it is vital that the curriculum offer our students receive fits their needs. Let's take a look at what that entails.

The new key judgement that involves curriculum is the 'Quality of Education' judgement. It is split into three key areas:

1. Intent: The curriculum you intend to offer your students.
  - What do leaders intend to offer to inspire young people?
  - Is the curriculum knowledge rich?
  - Is the curriculum developing students' cultural capital?
  - Is the curriculum broad and balanced?
  - Does the curriculum provide a range of subjects?
  - Is the curriculum coherent and well-sequenced?

2. Implementation: How you choose to deliver your curriculum.
  - Do all teachers understand the curriculum intent?
  - Do all teachers have strong subject knowledge?
  - Do all teachers present the content well?
  - Is there an effective and systemic assessment policy?
  - Is feedback timely and effective?
  - Are effective recall and retrieval systems in place?
  - Do all teachers teach responsively?

3. Impact: What is the impact of your curriculum?
  - What does the data tell you about progress and impact?
  - To what extent does your curriculum meet the interests of your learners?
  - To what extent does the curriculum match the aspirations of your learners?
  - To what extent does the curriculum match the intentions of your students' course of study?

It's important to notice the shift here. The emphasis isn't solely on academic success. This is a welcome change from the data-driven focus of bygone years. It means leaders can really focus on what is right in the context of their school and the students within it. If you haven't already reviewed your curriculum, now is the time. A curriculum that meets the needs of your individual students will be sure to pave the way for their success as well as promote well-rounded young people ready to enter the next stage of their lives. What an exciting time to be leading education!

Next steps

Time to review your curriculum offer? Why not meet with the subject leads to hash out a plan?

#curriculumcare
#learning

Idea 80: School counsellor

Having a school counsellor is vital in ensuring students who are potentially at risk are professionally supported, nurtured and kept safe.

There has been an increase in the number of young people experiencing worrying and sometimes serious mental health issues. The pressures upon young people are many: exam pressure, family problems, body image and identity concerns, social media pressure; the list goes on. The statistics involving young people and mental health are alarming. Mental health problems affect one in ten young people. 50 per cent of mental health problems are established by age 14 and 75 per cent by age 24. 70 per cent of children and young people who experience a mental health problem have not had appropriate interventions at a sufficiently early age. Therefore, it is vital that schools invest in the services of a school counsellor.

What are the benefits of having a school counsellor?

The British Association for Counselling and Psychotherapy (BACP) has explicitly stated the benefits of having school counsellors as part of any school's plan. They believe doing so has the following benefits:

- School-based counselling can stop mental health problems from developing further – this early intervention treatment can stop conditions accelerating into something more serious and complex, and offer children the tools to recognise when they are experiencing difficulties with their mental wellbeing.
- School-based counselling is easy for children to access – children and young people are seen usually in two to three weeks; it would be unusual to wait longer than four weeks to be assessed by a school counsellor.
- Children and young people are more likely to see an in-house school-based counsellor compared to non-school-based services; it cuts down their fears of stigma.
- School-based counselling helps with behaviour and learning.

- School-based counselling works as a parallel support alongside CAMHS and reduces referrals to these specialist and costly services.
- School-based counselling is cost effective. One session of CAMHS costs the same as five sessions of school counselling.

With these benefits in mind, it is easy to see why a school counsellor is so important to protect some of our vulnerable students. I would strongly argue the point with any headteacher that the benefits of having a school counsellor far outweigh the potential savings made by not including them in budget costings.

#schoolcounsellor
#connect
#notice

Idea 81: Student surveys

Student surveys are a great way to gauge the way students are truly feeling.

If you want to develop and promote wellbeing in schools, it is important to understand how the student body in your school genuinely feels. Student surveys can be a powerful tool to do this because:

- They are quick and efficient.
- They allow leaders to gather in-depth data on a large scale.
- They provide insightful information crucial to deciding next steps.
- They encourage honest responses if conducted anonymously.
- They allow students to feel their opinions are valued.
- They encourage students to trust that school leaders are committed to their education and wellbeing.
- They promote effective communication in schools and help students to develop these skills.

How should the survey be planned?

Firstly, decide upon the aim of the survey. If it is to get an understanding of how the students feel about all aspects of school, the survey could be completed in sections: lessons, breaktime, quality of resources, etc. If it's something more precise, like their views on equality and inclusivity, consider how the questions will be grouped. Our wonderful equality and diversity lead is brilliant at this! Next, compile a list of questions you intend to ask. Ensure they are clear and that the answers given will give you the information you need to analyse the results. Multiple choice questions are the easiest way to analyse data on such a large scale, but it can also be necessary to include some open comment sections for questions requiring a more developed response. Once questions have been carefully planned and considered, it's time to input them onto a survey site.

How should the survey be completed?

The best option is for students to take part anonymously on a site such as Survey Monkey or Google Forms. This ensures honesty and provides more reliable results.

#studentsurvey

Idea 82: Equality and inclusivity lead

Having a designated equality and inclusivity lead ensures all students are celebrated and included each year no matter what their differences.

Here at Whitefield School, where I work, we have an equality and diversity lead who is simply incredible. Lynmara Hingston, who also runs our very popular, bustling library, works hard all year round on making sure both staff and students alike are aware of each other's differences. Her work is especially important at Whitefield as we have an enormously diverse student and staff body with over 72 different languages spoken. Some of the ways in which she undertakes the role are listed below.

Student club: Spectrum

This is a club run by Lynmara every week. Students attend after school to discuss all things LGBTQ+. They are involved in whole-school events throughout the year too. Lynmara has created a space for young people to be themselves without fear of being judged. It is a real joy to see so many students attending the club and feeling welcomed by everyone who attends.

Diversity Week

This is a huge national event that many schools take part in. It is a chance for the school to annually come together to support and raise awareness of the issues affecting those in the LGBTQ+ community. The week involves the entire school coming together to celebrate being you. The final day is called Rainbow Day, where Year 7 students are invited to take part in games, poetry, face painting, arts and crafts and much more. It is a day thoroughly enjoyed by all. This celebration continues with a student trip to Pride in London. A small number of students are selected to go to this event as a reward for their contributions to equality and inclusivity across the year. Staff buy special rainbow lanyards to wear in celebration too. All proceeds are sent off to a relevant charity.

Women's History Month

This event is spread across an entire month. It once again involves the entire school. Posters of inspirational women, nominated by staff, are shared all over the school for their notable successes. Tutor time activities are planned and delivered. They involve creative activities, competitions and informative videos all about wonderful women. It's a great month of celebration.

Movember

In November there is a focus on men, in particular men's health. Once again, there are various ways in which we celebrate and fundraise. This year, it involved staff giving moustache stickers to any male students who had demonstrated positive role model behaviours. There was a walking challenge to raise money, and of course, our male staff members are encouraged to grow their own moustache for a month in order to raise funds.

World Mental Health Day

Aside from a week of activities for World Mental Health Awareness, our Wellbeing Lead, Ewa Micun, works with Lynmara and other members of staff in organising World Mental Health Day, which is always a great event. Everyone is encouraged to wear yellow to raise awareness and money for the charity Young Minds.

School assemblies

Lynmara presents these along with James Clarke, our lively, effervescent drama teacher. Assemblies are used to raise awareness of the issues mentioned above, as well as any other topics that the leads feel it necessary to discuss. Students are taught about the importance of accepting each other, about values of tolerance, respect and equality, and about how they should be mindful of the language they use when discussing different groups in society.

Tutor time

Tutor time activities are regularly planned to raise awareness for a whole host of topics from World Mental Health Day, where we also encourage everyone to wear yellow and donate to charity, Black

History Month, LGBT+ History Month, Disabilities History Month, Women's History Month and Neurodiversity Week.

As well as these wonderful celebration days, Lynmara also works hard on ensuring that equality is consistent across the school on a day-to-day basis. Important work is undertaken and delivered to staff on a regular basis. Some of that work includes whole-school surveys on various equality issues such as racism and homophobia. The surveys are then checked against school behavioural records to identify patterns of behaviour and discrepancies in the data. This work encourages staff to be more aware of their own potential unconscious bias and to be more sensitive with regards to young people and their understanding of who they are. Each year, CPD is delivered with regards to the most up-to-date information on equality and inclusivity. These sessions are not only informative, but incredibly thought-provoking. They challenge staff to be aware of their own prejudices and encourage everyone to be mindful of how they deal with negative behaviours from students towards specific groups within our school community. By having leads work continuously throughout the year on such sensitive issues, it ensures a commitment from all stakeholders towards a harmonious, inclusive and accepting community. It also prepares our young people for the diverse world in which they live.

Next steps

Why not create your own equality and inclusivity leads in your school or if that is not an option, consider celebrating diversity in one of the ways listed above? Perhaps, you could run a club that promotes equality and inclusivity across the school?

#equalityandinclusivity
#connect
#learn
#notice

Idea 83: Whole-school peer mentoring

Allowing young people to mentor their peers can yield powerful results.

Liam Davis, a teacher at Woodside High, Wood Green, London, shares his idea about peer mentoring below.

One of the most powerful interventions I've seen is the intervention of a peer mentor. Sometimes young people find it easier to open up to people their own age rather than adults. If those young people are empowered with the training to become a mentor they can carry out the role with great authority. By encouraging students to become mentors you will be asking them to work on their own personal skills, getting them to think about reflection, self-esteem and confidence. This simple programme is a way of supporting student wellbeing.

To start, mentors need to be selected. One way of doing this is to launch it in assembly to students. Historically, Year 10 is a good year to pitch this to, although you could use it with Year 11 and Year 13. Post assembly, an application process can begin whereby students need to complete an application form which details why they should become a mentor coupled with, for example, how many achievement or behaviour points they have accumulated in that academic year.

Those chosen can then be invited for an interview with a senior member of staff or the pastoral team. In the interview, ask questions around mentoring and how they would apply it. I always ask: 'How would you deal with a situation if you saw a friend steal a mobile phone?' Students who interview well can then undergo training. Students take part in four sessions:

1. **What makes a good mentor?** Trainee mentors think about the skills and qualities needed to be a good mentor – such as confidence, trust and respect.
2. **Stereotypes and assumptions.** Trainee mentors think about how to challenge stereotypes and the roots of assumptions that students make all too often about each other. They also think how to

tackle inequality so that each student starts with a level playing field despite how their behaviour may have been.

3. **Communication and diversity.** Trainee mentors think about how to set targets for their mentees and track and monitor targets each week. Trainees also reflect on the best and worst experiences of their life and whether having a mentor would have helped them.

4. **Safeguarding and confidentiality.** In the final session trainee mentors look at safeguarding. This session is delivered either by an external safeguarding organisation or the designated safeguarding lead. Questions such as, 'What are some of the safeguarding issues that may arise?' are posed. They look at issues such as self-harm, abuse and neglect, how to look for tell-tale signs and how the reporting process works. Additionally they look at which issues in their relationship with their mentee they can keep confidential and which they cannot. Stress is placed upon them understanding that anything that is a safeguarding risk must be reported to the appropriate adult in school.

You can ask mentors to complete an assessment on finishing training. When all this is completed, students can be presented with a badge and tie to recognise their achievement of becoming a mentor. Then the mentoring can begin. If you choose Year 10 as your mentors, generally Years 7 to 9 will be their mentees. If Year 11 are your mentors Years 7 to 10 may be your mentees. If you operate it in the sixth form with Year 13 as your mentors, Years 11 and 12 may be your mentees.

Once this has been established, the mentors and mentees can begin their professional relationship. Mentors complete a record sheet which records the conversation and targets set by the mentor for their mentee. This is then reviewed the following week. Mentors can liaise with tutors and teachers to see how their mentee is doing, as well as put them on direct report to them.

When they have more experience, mentors can take on more responsibility, for example, going to the local primary school to read with students, presenting assemblies on good mental health to the rest of the school and acting as ambassadors at whole-school events. Something so simple to set up can be very powerful.

Next steps
Think about which year group to pitch this to depending on the age range of your school. Set up the application process and look at how to arrange your training.

#peermentoring
#connect
#volunteer

Idea 84: Whole-school rewards

Rewarding students for positive behaviour reinforces the desired behaviour.

No school is complete without a whole-school reward system. This is a chance for the entire school community to come together and celebrate the positive behaviours of all students. In order for a whole-school rewards system to work, it must be:

- consistent across the entire school
- not too time-consuming for staff
- linked solely to positive behaviours and separate from sanctions
- publicly acknowledged, with parents informed too
- personally accrued, so each student can see their contribution
- simple for tutors to visually share
- inexpensive to run.

Every school has a rewards system, but I believe some are more effective than others at promoting positive behaviour. Below are some examples of reward systems that I have seen used both in schools I have worked in and in schools across the country.

Student of the month

This is a great way for students to be recognised for their efforts each month. Year leads or heads of house each nominate students who they feel have worked hard, have contributed to the school and deserve recognition. Students are then invited to the headteacher's office for drinks and snacks and an informal discussion about what they like about the school and what they'd like to see improved. It's a great way for young people to have their voices heard. We have a student of the month display in reception, so all students' names and photographs are displayed there too.

House or year group point system

Students accumulate points for positive behaviour and at the end of each term or year, prizes are awarded for the tutor group/house/year group with the most points. Students love the element of competition and it's a lovely way to end each half term or term on a high. Most schools have a points-based system in place to reward students, but the best examples I have seen is where a visual is provided too. In some schools, they have installed tubes to represent each house or year group. Students are given tokens for excellent behaviour and these are put into the tubes. It's a brilliant way for students to track their progress, whilst promoting better effort from those wanting to win. In a previous school I worked at, each house had a mascot. Tutor groups who won the most points each week were given the mascot to take care of in their classroom. The excitement this generates is a joy to behold, even with the older Year 10s and 11s! Leader boards are another great way to display the efforts of students.

Rewards trips

These are a great way to reward students whose behaviour has been exemplary all year. In my school, the Student of the Month Award also includes a trip. This can be to a museum or notable places of interest or to something like ice skating or bowling. We also have end-of-year rewards trips for entire year groups depending on their collective effort across the year. Whilst there is some debate about whether rewards trips exclude those who never get the chance to experience trips, as long as there are opportunities for all students to go on one elsewhere in the school calendar, I see no reason not to reward those students who are deserving of a special outing.

Leaders

Having house captains or year group leaders ensures that students are involved in the rewards planning and delivery. This level of student involvement is important as students feel they are included in some key decisions about how the school is run and which rewards to offer their peers. Each year, the leaders are changed through a new application process and it is a chance for some new students to become involved.

Next steps

Why not review the whole-school rewards policy in your school? Is it effective? Do students value it? If not, what can you do to renew and reinvigorate the system?

#wholeschoolrewards
#connect

Idea 85: Tidy timetable

A sensible timetable plan ensures both students and teachers have a balanced week.

A contentious time in any school year is when new timetables are distributed. This can cause either tension and chaos at the beginning of a new school year or a pleasantly calm start with few hiccups. To achieve the latter, some careful steps should take place.

Step 1: Decide on the important decisions as a leadership team in the spring term. Questions like: do we want double lessons this year? If so, which subjects have requested them in the past? Which subjects shall we place back-to-back on the timetable? Does it make sense to have the core subjects in the same blocks? These decisions are crucial to the smooth transitioning of the timetable. They also make class swaps and student class moves easier (or more difficult).

Step 2: Direct middle leaders in the summer term. Inform heads of department of your non-negotiable timetable requests and ask them to organise their own requests well in advance. A good deadline would be May half term. This gives the timetable creator plenty of time.

Step 3: Allow the timetable creator time to complete the task. The role of timetable creator is not envied by many in schools, not least because of the mammoth task of formulating the information shared by the middle leaders. There are bound to be problems that need communicating with leaders before any decisions can be made. Thus, plenty of time is needed for things to run smoothly.

Step 4: Share the completed timetables with staff before the end of term. This step is crucial in ensuring that both staff and students alike are given the best possible start to the new academic year. I have worked in schools where teachers haven't been given the timetable until the first day of teaching. This is stressful for all involved. By handing out timetables in the summer term, staff can plan effective and challenging lessons suited to the students in their class well in advance.

#tidytimetable

Idea 86: Wellbeing lead

Creating a wellbeing lead in school encourages a focus on wellbeing all year round.

Many schools might not see the wellbeing role as one they can commit to with the current financial constraints schools are under, but here are a few reasons why creating this role is worth it.

- It ensures wellbeing is a focus throughout the year.
- A wellbeing lead has time to plan events that specifically tie in to the school's improvement plan. They can also seek out funding available to schools through various national projects or charities.
- Students know there is always someone they can talk to if they need.

What type of activities and events can the wellbeing lead organise?

- **Trips:** Our wellbeing lead (Ewa Micun) ensures that there are regular opportunities for school trips. She seeks out funding grants and secures them, which means that no student is left behind.
- **Surveys:** Regular surveys are planned and completed. These surveys can be about road safety, travel and transport or general wellbeing. They offer important insights into the lives of the students we serve.
- **Charity events:** Throughout the year, charity events are organised by the wellbeing lead to raise funds. Our wellbeing lead does an excellent job with this, particularly when it comes to baking cakes!
- **Assemblies:** Ewa also spends time delivering assemblies on important topics varying from extracurricular activities to bullying.
- **Wellbeing highlights:** Ewa plans much smaller events throughout the year. A recent example was a 'thank you' display board in the canteen. Students could pin a note to the board for everyone to see.

This is obviously not an exhaustive list, but I hope it is enough to get you thinking about what the role could entail in your school. We are certainly very grateful to our wonderful Ewa!

#wellbeingwinning
#notice

Next steps
Why not set up a wellbeing committee in your school? That way you could investigate any potential candidates for such a role and take it from there.

Idea 87: Animal magic

Caring for animals has many benefits for students and staff alike.

Below are some of the benefits of having animals in your school.

- **They reduce stress.** Research in the US has proven that people who own pets are less stressed when conducting certain tasks if their pets are with them during the task.
- **They improve mood.** Pets really can improve a person's mood. This is one of the main reasons pets are used in different types of therapy. In some cases, dogs are used to help soldiers recover from post-traumatic stress disorder, for example.
- **They improve socialisation skills.** Owning pets actually improves socialisation skills, as they lead people into situations in which they will have to interact with others.
- **They prevent allergies and improve immunity.** Research has proven that owning pets as a young child actually prevents allergies later on in life.
- **They support emotional development.** Pets help pupils develop emotionally as they learn how to express themselves and empathise better. The sensory aspect of pet care also supports pupils with autism.
- **They build a sense of responsibility.** For pupils with attention deficit hyperactivity disorder (ADHD), pet care can encourage them to be responsible through caring and an effective routine. Likewise, all pupils can learn how to take care of another life through care of animals at school.

I know schools that are real animal havens with alpacas in the school field and visiting lambs during spring. Many schools now have school dogs too. If you aren't able to go to these lengths in your school, why not have a small school pet – a rabbit or even some stick insects – that students are encouraged to take care of and show responsibility towards?

Alternatively, you could take students to the animals. There are many open farms across the country who welcome school visits. My school offers something called Equine Therapy. Some of our most vulnerable students are taken to Strength and Learning Through Horses in North London each term to learn how to care for horses. It's an amazing opportunity for them to be with animals, learn about responsibility and improve their mental health.

> **Next steps**
> Why not encourage responsibility even further by allowing pupils to take pets home over half term to care for? You could even allow pupils the opportunity to look after the animals during break and lunch on rotation depending on what kind of animals you have in the school.

#animalmagic
#connect
#volunteer
#learn
#exercise

Idea 88: Transitions to secondary school

Moving from primary to secondary school involves a degree of apprehension for most pupils. Pupils have to adapt to a more challenging school setting with different academic structures and expectations as well as changes in social interactions.

Kelly Hannaghan, Wellbeing Lead at Lessness Heath Primary School, Belvedere, London (part of The Primary First Trust) shares her ideas on how to make transition effective and stress free for primary pupils.

A successful transition involves functioning well in two areas:

- being academically and behaviourally involved in school
- feeling a sense of belonging to school.

Secondary schools are generally much larger than primary schools, the setting is very different with pupils being placed in classes that are set by academic ability, with much more movement around the school environment. In order for pupils to feel secure during the transition period the following ideas should be considered.

Partnerships with parents

Parents are an important source of support over the transition period. It can be helpful for parents and pupils to discuss their concerns. Creating leaflets with some practical suggestions of how to do this can really help. Inviting parents to transition meetings both within the primary and secondary schools can help build the bridge and overcome any anxieties around the upcoming change. Children's psychological adjustment, their relationships with peers and the interface between school and the family environment is vital to get right.

Home information gathering can help a pupil's wellbeing when transitioning to secondary school. Asking primary schools for information about a child's parents and home background can be a key indicator of needs. It's important to ask questions about levels of parental support.

Here are some of pupils' common concerns around the transition to secondary school.

Top pupil concerns

Before transition (in Year 6 of primary school):

- getting lost
- being bullied
- discipline and detentions
- homework
- losing old friends.

After transition (beginning of Year 7 in secondary school):

- losing old friends
- discipline and detentions
- homework
- getting lost
- older children
- being bullied.

Primary and secondary links

Identifying factors that predict successful and difficult transitions to secondary school is vital. These could be highlighted by offering student surveys in Year 6 of primary and Year 7 of secondary.

There are a variety of ways to collect pupil voice including full online emotional health questionnaires such as SEPQs (Social, Emotional, Profile Questionnaires) or SDQs (Strength and Difficulty Questionnaires). Alternatively, you could simply take snap shots, by asking three simple questions:

1. Where would you rate your overall wellbeing on a scale of one to ten?
2. What do you need to support your wellbeing?
3. What is the biggest barrier to you feeling emotionally well?

These questions could be asked at different times throughout the school year. These can be particularly helpful at pinch points, for example around settling in periods. It is important to discuss with students general feedback from the surveys, with a strategy and actions to show you are taking pupils' voices seriously and acting upon needs.

The use of systemic strategies in primary schools is also important, involving building links and continuity between primary and secondary school, such as by using bridging units – work projects that children begin in primary school and complete in secondary school. Secondary school strategies include a range of practices that can be employed to support friendships, as this is an area of persistent concern for pupils.

Organise special days in the new secondary school to provide the students with an opportunity to familiarise themselves with the new environment. It may be that vulnerable pupils need additional taster days to help alleviate any anxieties. Ensure support is put in place for pupils who have been identified by their primary schools as having additional social needs or anxieties.

Provide an emotionally available adult for vulnerable pupils

Young people can be at their most vulnerable when transitioning to secondary school: they have feelings of loss from leaving their primary schools and may even have left behind stable and safe relationships with their peers and educators. Providing vulnerable children with daily access to at least one named, emotionally available adult who believes in them helps regulate young people with compassion, empathy and unconditional positive regard.

What are the benefits of having an adult mentor?

- It provides appropriate limit setting, understanding of their attachment and mental health needs, and offers repeated enriched relational, regulatory and reflective opportunities.
- It ensures that young people are caught as they are 'falling', not after they have fallen. When the pupil is experiencing a painful life event, the emotionally available adults will help them process, work through and make sense of what has happened.

- Staff are trained in the art of good listening, understanding and finding the words to convey accurate empathy.
- It creates a commitment to relating to children in a school or other setting in ways that help them feel calm, soothed and safe.
- Staff and adults interact with all children in such a way that they feel valued as individuals throughout their day.
- Staff and adults adjust their expectations of vulnerable children to correspond with their developmental capabilities and experience of traumatic stress.

Transitions can be the most challenging times in a young person's life. Coupled with the extensive brain development at this time, it's important for schools to provide a consistent and safe environment for these moments within a child's life.

#transitioncare
#connect
#notice

Idea 89: The importance of PSHE

PSHE lessons are an important aspect of any school curriculum and should not be seen as a tag on to the more traditional subjects in schools.

The PSHE Association states that, 'PSHE education is a school subject through which pupils develop the knowledge, skills and attributes they need to keep themselves healthy and safe, and prepared for life and work. Well-delivered PSHE programmes have an impact on both academic and non-academic outcomes for pupils, particularly the most vulnerable and disadvantaged.' PSHE stands for personal, social, health and economic education and here's why it is important. It provides students with skills they need to keep themselves healthy and safe, whilst preparing them for life and work in the UK. It supports their wellbeing and tackles issues that can affect their ability to learn, such as anxiety and unhealthy relationships. It is a legal requirement for all schools to include a PSHE curriculum.

How to get PSHE right

- Treat PSHE in the same way that other subjects are treated. It should be timetabled in the same way – the official guidance is one hour per week of PSHE education in Key Stages 1–4. A whole-school approach would further enhance students' learning.
- PSHE should be taught as discrete lessons. Although many subjects may well contribute to the same aims as PSHE lessons, such as students' personal and social development, it is important for students' understanding and recognition of its importance that it remains a separate subject.
- A cross-curricular approach is difficult to manage due to a lack of continuity and of an overview of progression, and problems when seeking meaningful assessment. Discrete lessons avoid these issues.
- The PSHE curriculum should be built in the same way that other subject curriculums are considered. It should build on previously acquired knowledge and students should be provided with regular feedback on their progress.

It is not difficult to understand why some schools have chosen not to follow these guidelines. In today's education system, schools are under unprecedented pressure to get results that count. League tables, tight funding, continuous educational reform and change at government level have led to a system of managerialism that forces school leaders to make changes they may not have been entirely happy with. However, PSHE lessons must remain a priority or we risk the wellbeing of our students.

For more support and guidance on all things PSHE-related, I urge school leaders to take a look at the PSHE Association's website and perhaps become a member. It is full of sensible advice on the importance of the subject as well as advice and guidance on how to implement an effective PSHE curriculum. Find out more here: www.pshe-association.org.uk.

#PSHEpower
#studentwellbeingmatters
#getitright

Idea 90: External wellbeing resources

Seeking support to embed a wellbeing policy in schools ensures student wellbeing is a priority.

Sometimes knowing where to begin with a whole-school focus on wellbeing can be a daunting problem. If school leaders are not sure about how to implement wellbeing support for young people, then any strategies incorporated can seem tokenistic or ill thought through. Before thinking about introducing systems to support student wellbeing, it can be a good idea to seek support from external professional networks. The two mental health charities below are a good place to begin. Both share advice on whole-school wellbeing approaches.

Young Minds

Young Minds is a charity committed to fighting for a future where all young minds are supported and empowered, whatever the challenges. They have four strategic aims:

1. Foster innovation to meet the needs of vulnerable and excluded children and young people.
2. Promote good mental health to more children and young people than ever before.
3. Champion the voices of young people and parents to influence mental health policy and practice.
4. Inspire excellence to achieve transformed, integrated services.

They launched 360° Schools as part of their mission. It's a programme that helps leaders to put wellbeing at the heart of their schools' improvement. As part of the 360° Schools' Community, school leaders receive e-newsletters packed with free teaching resources, videos, tips and examples of good practice in mental health and wellbeing from other professionals. They also offer bespoke training and support to schools in-house and a consultancy service to help school leaders commission, design and deliver better mental health interventions and services that generate the outcomes that matter to children, young people and families.

You can find out more at the website: www.youngminds.org.uk.

Heads Together

Heads Together is a charity that has launched the Mentally Healthy Schools whole-school wellbeing approach. Although it is aimed at primary schools primarily, their website contains many free resources and comprehensive advice on how to develop wellbeing in schools. They believe that a whole-school approach is about developing a positive ethos and culture – where everyone feels that they belong. It involves working with families and making sure that the whole-school community is welcoming, inclusive and respectful. It means maximising children's learning through promoting good mental health and wellbeing across the school – through the curriculum, support for pupils, staff–pupil relationships, leadership and a commitment from everybody. They have an online resources library that school leaders can access for support. They also offer ten tips for whole-school wellbeing development.

1. Provide clear leadership, vision, strategy and plans for improvement.
2. Develop a school policy for mental health and wellbeing.
3. Create a warm and supportive environment.
4. Create a culture where mental health can be talked about openly.
5. Weave PSHE topics throughout the curriculum.
6. Develop strategies to support at-risk children.
7. Guide staff on how to refer a child.
8. Work with families and communities.
9. Protect children from harm and neglect.
10. Support staff mental health and wellbeing.

You can find out more by visiting their website:
www.mentallyhealthyschools.org.uk.

Another place you can look for support is the service below.

Healthy Schools

Healthy Schools is a health and wellbeing service that offers support and advice to schools nationally. They support schools to raise attainment and achievement by improving the health and wellbeing of pupils. They aim to achieve this through working together with schools to offer an effective, evidence-based online School Health Check tool, available to schools and school settings nationally and internationally.

Here is some more information about the School Health Check:

- The tool ensures schools have the fundamental elements of Healthy Schools in place to achieve and maintain Healthy School Status.
- It allows schools to audit health and wellbeing across all four themes and grade provision using Ofsted-style descriptors to identify and celebrate strengths, as well as next steps.
- Each 'criteria' has been matched, wherever possible, to current Ofsted descriptors, therefore helping schools to understand the links between health and wellbeing and Ofsted.
- Schools will also need to identify a target for each of the four health themes. These targets can be used to inform next steps and working towards the Health Champion model which demonstrates impact and improvement over a period of time.

You can find out more at their website: www.healthyschools.org.uk.

Next steps

Why not review your own school's wellbeing policy? Or if you don't have one, start by looking at the online resources available above and plan how to make your own school a mentally healthy place for students.

#healthyschools
#wholeschoolwellbeing

Index